# Learning Can Stick

## A GUIDE TO MAKE EVERY LEARNING EXPERIENCE SAFE, LOGICAL, FUN, AND MEMORABLE

# DR. CHRISTIE L. McMULLEN

For permission requests and ordering information, email the publisher at:
info@twopennypublishing.com

Illustrations by: Emily Byrd
Handwriting Illustrations by: Chloe McMullen
Book Cover by: Adrian Traurig
Book Design by: Jodi Costa

ISBN: 978-1-950995-15-8
eBook also available

FIRST EDITION

For more information about this author or to book event appearance or media interview, please contact the author representative at:
info@twopennypublishing.com

Make work fun
So people don't
quit!

♡,
Christie

Wonderful!

To anyone who has ever stood in front of a group of people
in an effort to teach them something.
May this book give you some new tools for your tool belt.

# CONTENTS

# Introduction

Bueller?

Bueller?

In 1986, we all heard those words come out of a terribly boring teacher's mouth and absolutely no one was listening. The class was focused on anything but this man and his roll call. *Ferris Bueller's Day Off* might be too old a reference for some of you, but the truth of that cinematic moment rings true in all learning opportunities. If you haven't ever seen it, add it to your watch list!

As a facilitator/teacher/parent/presenter, if you do not capture the attention of your audience, you might as well be speaking to an empty room.

Welcome to *Learning Can Stick: A guide to help you make every learning experience safe, logical, fun, and memorable.*

I will be your guide for this adventure; but you, my friend, will be the hero. By the end of this book, you will know how to entice people to gain knowledge in your presence.

You might be a physical therapist who works with patients one on one, and you need the patient to understand their protocol of exercises; or, a corporate trainer who travels the country working with participants from multi-million dollar corporations, teaching them about compliance or the latest sales techniques. Regardless, these strategies will enhance your already awesome style.

If you guide the work of others in any capacity, but particularly if you facilitate professional learning, this book has tips and tricks for you. If you want your participants to leave your sessions knowing more than they did when they came, and to utilize new learning over the long haul, this book is for you.

For 20+ years, I have studied and practiced in the area of teaching and learning. I have learned some great tools and tricks, and I am excited to share them with you. I will work through how to use these new tools so your participants leave your time together with learning that will last.

As humans, we are constantly learning. Some things we choose to learn because they interest us, like playing a guitar or doing woodworking. Other things we learn out of necessity for our careers, like sales tactics and spreadsheet tips and tricks. When learning something we want to learn, we pay full attention. We cannot wait to study the subject, find new ways to experience it, and grow in that area.

As a facilitator, you may face the challenge of making the needed learning become the wanted learning.

The strategies in this book have been honed over two decades of experiences and opportunities and will help you. In those two decades I have experienced many "Bueller" moments as a learner; and because I know what not to do, I have mastered what to do to make sure those moments never happen when I am teaching. I want to share that insight with you through some practical and easily repeatable steps.

I can't do that until we establish what it means for learning to be *sticky*.
Picture this:

## EXAMPLE 1:

Your grandmother has a fantastic pie crust recipe that has been passed down for generations. No one in your family has learned it yet, and you really want to be the one to do it. You ask your grandmother to teach you how to make the perfect pie crust. She is patient with you, and you hang on her every word as you work to learn all the nuances of her recipe. You watch intently, ask questions, and practice after you are done, to make sure you remember all you learned. She shows you more than once, and she encourages you when you make mistakes. This learning had stickiness.

It was something you wanted to learn and can now do.

In example 1, your grandmother listened and was patient. She modeled expectations and worked alongside you. You wanted to learn the material and were attentive as she taught you.

The learning was sticky because the facilitator and the learner worked together to make the learning stick.

## EXAMPLE 2:

You attend mandatory training in sales techniques. You are a salesperson and really want to learn new ways of work. The trainer did the majority of the talking, and there were no opportunities to practice the new techniques. You did not feel comfortable asking questions, and you found your mind wandering a bit. When you went on your next sales call, you tried one of the new techniques; but it did not go particularly well. You no longer use what you learned in the workshop. This learning did not have stickiness. It was something you wanted to learn, but the learning didn't stick; and you aren't quite sure what to do with the information.

In example 2, the trainer had lots of great information but did the majority of the talking; he did not model expectations nor let the participant wrestle with the information. You wanted to learn the material and were attentive but not involved.

The learning was not sticky because the facilitator did not involve the learner in the learning.

## EXAMPLE 3:

You attend a mandatory training about CPR. You have been in the medical field for 20 years and are very comfortable with the process. You were sure this was going to be a waste of your time. The trainer began by asking about the expertise in the room. He realized there was a strong understanding of CPR already. Instead of going through the basics, the trainer used the brilliance in the room to deepen the learning of all participants. You role played, leaving the training with lots of fresh ideas on how you could better serve patients if CPR were necessary, as well as how to help with breathing issues and high-stress situations. This learning did have stickiness. It was not something you wanted to learn, but you did, despite not being sure you needed or wanted to do so.

In example 3, the trainer listened to the learner and adjusted the structure accordingly. The participant did not want to learn, but did so in spite of the desire not to. The participant did not intend for the learning to stick, but it did anyway.

The learning was sticky because the facilitator involved the learners and listened to their needs. After adjusting the training to meet the learner needs, the learning stuck.

It is possible to use the learning in other situations when it sticks. That means remembering the new information beyond just memorization. Learning that sticks changes the way we do things or improves on existing skills.

Learning lasts when the trainer evokes interest in the content, and the learning environment engages the learner. When the content is engaging, and the delivery method requires action from the learner, people will remember what you taught.

The "you" in this book will be you, the facilitator; but that does not mean there is an us-against-them mentality with the learner. To be a great facilitator, it is imperative to think like the learners and meet their needs. Gramma worked with you to make sure the pie recipe became your own, bringing you into the learning experience as a true participant. The CPR trainer listened and made the opportunity relevant to the audience, working with the learners instead of assuming all knowledge lay within. The sales trainer tried to do it alone, leaving the participant behind, bored, and frustrated.

In a perfect world, the learner is willing, the facilitator is amazing, and the learning sticks. In the real world, your sphere of influence is larger than your sphere of control. You cannot, as the facilitator, control the learner's desire to retain the information; but you can control the way you deliver the information to increase the stickiness.

In every circumstance, there is a sphere of influence and sphere of control. The sphere of control is typically small. You might be able to control the temperature of the room or the length of time you get to meet with participants, but the list of true control is relatively short. The sphere of influence is much larger and can span a larger swath of circumstances. You can influence how people feel in your session, how much or how little gets covered, what information gets used after the training ends, and other bigger results. ***Focus on your sphere of influence to get participants to buy into your learning opportunity.***

Every learning experience has the potential to be potent enough to last in the learner's mind.

If the facilitator makes the environment safe, logical, fun, and memorable, the learner and the facilitator reach the goal of a positive experience.

There should be:
- clear direction
- engagement
- relevance of content
- processing time

Throughout this book, I will walk through the experiences that achieve stickiness of learning. You might work with people one on one, or train large groups. Either way, the ideas in this book will work.

If you make the learning *safe*, building authenticity and clarity, learning will stick.

If you make the learning *logical*, the learner's mind can retain the content and learning will stick.

If you make the learning *fun*, the learner will feel valued and celebrated, and learning will stick.

If you make the learning *memorable*, the accountability and follow up will make learning stick.

## HOW TO READ THIS BOOK:

I will be using trickery and shenanigans disguised as learning practices throughout this book to model how to make learning stick. The more you engage with those practices, the more likely you will be to use the new strategies in your next training session.

Each chapter will begin with a list of "need to know" items outlining what you will learn in that section. This list will help guide your learning.

Each chapter ends with three things:

# NEED TO KNOW

A review of the chapter objectives

# NOTE-TAKING

Suggested synthesis and capturing techniques

# NEXT STEPS

What should you do with the information?

When you write things down, you have involved your brain and your body, which helps, but does not work for everyone. Our pastor says 90% of people who take notes get into Heaven though, so I will let you decide what to do.

Let's work as a team to avoid the "Bueller" moments. Instead go for the Michelle Pfieffer from *Dangerous Minds* moments. Make learning stick at all costs because your participants deserve the best.

# CHAPTER 1

# The Power of Making Learning Stick

## NEED TO KNOW

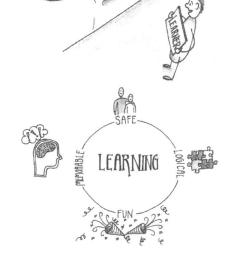

- Focus on the adult learner and the why of learning.

- Make learning safe, logical, fun, and memorable.

- Spend significant time in the learning zone.

- Embrace and evoke change.

Anyone can sing karaoke, but let's be clear—not everyone should. I love watching karaoke when it is done well. The people who are best at karaoke are the ones who do it to have fun, not necessarily to show off Grammy-award-winning vocals.

Have you ever sung along with the radio and thought, "Dang, I sound good."? Or maybe you are a shower singer, where the acoustics are just right, and you and Nicki Minaj sound exactly alike. We have all done it, and somehow we think that amazing sound will translate to a karaoke opportunity.

Allow me to let you in on a little secret. It sounds MUCH better in your head.

That said, there are ways to win at karaoke.

1.  **Know your limits.** Mariah Carey is the only one who can actually hit those notes. Leave that to her. Make a safer choice.

2.  **Timing matters.** Free Bird is never a good idea. Keep it short and leave them wanting more.

3.  **Involve the audience.** Sweet Caroline works every time because we all love to do the ba, ba, ba. Admit it, you just sang it in your head.

4.  **Choose a song everyone knows and loves.** Summer Nights has a line for everyone. Now is not the time to introduce an original.

These foolproof karaoke concepts will help you win with training too.

*Make it safe.* There is no need to hit all the high notes, but instead make sure that everyone feels like they can succeed in the environment you have created for them. Pull them in by making sure they see where and how they fit in the situation.

***Make it logical.*** Timing always matters. Build the experience to account for physical and emotional needs and know when people have met their limits. There is no need for the 11-minute guitar solo.

***Make it fun.*** Everyone loves a little audience participation. The person doing the talking is the person doing the learning, so let them "sing along." The fun evokes emotion, making the learning stick.

***Make it memorable.*** Trigger past experiences and get them to make connections throughout the learning. Put the "microphone" in their faces and give them a specific role to play. It is tough to forget it when you were the one who did it.

No one wants to be the "terrible-at-karaoke" girl and nobody wants to be the "can't-get-his-point-across" guy. Technique and practice are what prevents those from being our titles. As a communicator of information, i.e. trainer, manager, parent, friend, spouse, etc., we need to recognize our strengths and work to improve our weaknesses. The knowledge is there; the execution is what needs finesse.

Let's be honest. We have all attended a miserable training experience. The PowerPoint slides were read verbatim. The facilitator spoke in a monotone. The material was dry and uninteresting. The entire situation was downright painful. I bet you do not remember a single thing from that training. You were likely thinking, "I will never get those two hours of my life back." The singer picked Free Bird and happened to be tone deaf. And yet the trainer knew the information, he just lacked finesse.

What if I told you it did not have to be that way?

What if I told you even the most mundane material could be made engaging and fun?

Regardless of the profession, learning needs to happen; but the training experience is so often poorly executed, and therefore ineffective.

No more "Bueller" moments. No more wasted time. Let's get excited about the opportunity to make your learning experience the kind people cannot wait to attend. Adults want to know why something is important to them. The hook for adults is relevance.

I teach teachers, primarily. Yes, that is a thing. I help educators get better at what they do so that students have every opportunity to have a brighter future. Guess who are the absolute worst students...TEACHERS!

I have used the techniques in this book to convince the most set-in-their-ways educators that there is a better way to educate tiny humans. In doing so, I have mastered the art of getting adults to see relevance in improving how they deliver information.

No one wakes up in the morning and says, "I want to suck at my job today!" Sadly, we just don't have the tools to be successful...yet. The power of yet is that regardless of the current skill level or knowledge, "yet" means growth can happen.

Dr. Carol Dweck's work around growth mindset is especially relevant when working with adult learners. We have had lots more years to get "stuck" believing that we can't do things and have developed strong fixed mindsets.

"I am not a math person." "I can't cook." "I don't do mornings."

What if we added a yet to that?

"I am not a math person, YET." "I can't cook, YET." "I don't do mornings, YET."

*A growth mindset allows for a human to improve in an area.*
Creating a growth mindset in a learning opportunity takes finesse and skill on the part of the facilitator. The stage must be set for the needs of the learner to be met.

Recently, I joined a team tasked to design a digital training experience on an incredibly condensed timeline. Thanks a lot COVID. I was partnered with some brilliant women who had worked in the digital space for years. When we first started, they were running circles around me, and I was running like mad to try to keep up. They were throwing around words like Edji, Popplet, Nearpod, Google Slides, Padlet, Answer Garden, and I was over here waving my hands saying, "English, please!"

I decided, however, to have a growth mindset. I was not as tech savvy as they were, YET. They took the time to explain things to me in a language I could understand, and I was open-minded enough to listen.

As a learner, having a growth mindset changes everything; but you cannot control the learner. You can only make it safe for the participant to have that growth mindset. As the trainer, you create a space where asking questions gets praised, not knowing is acceptable, and the power of "yet" reigns.

Do you work with adults who need to learn the information you are delivering to improve job or life performance?

Is your delivery engaging for adult learners, allowing them to foster a growth mindset? Are there strategies to help you involve participants more in the learning?

Are you concerned the energy and passion you put into your session will not result in the ongoing use of the material by the participants?

Here is the secret formula. I am letting you peek behind the curtain.

Let's begin getting better together by reviewing the specific needs and characteristics of adult learners.

## ADULT LEARNING

Andragogy is the technical term for the art and science of adult education. It is a learner-centered approach for all ages, but really peaks when the learner decides he/she wants to learn.

For twenty years, I have dedicated myself to the art and science of learning. Although I started as a high school teacher, the majority of those twenty years were spent training adults. I have discovered some essential things about training adults and how to engage them in learning.

In any industry, continued education is required in some capacity. How well that learning sticks and ultimately alters behavior depends on two things: the delivery method used to teach the information and the learner's motivation to retain the information.

If done right, the delivery method can make learning stick even when the motivation of the learner is not as strong. Motivate the learner, and you have almost guaranteed a new skill set will be retained and utilized. Attending a required training does not equate to interest in the topic. It is often a struggle to get people to the training at all. They may feel it will be a waste of their time because the engagement level is low and the relevance is not clear. These issues can be resolved with intentional setup and explanation when the training begins.

If a person is "voluntold" to attend a training, buying into the learning opportunity is much less likely. Don't ignore this. This lack of buy in, instead, must be addressed. Content matters to adult learners, so it is imperative to communicate the direct impact of the information on the learner.

## RETURN ON INVESTMENT

Industries do not set out to simply waste money, time, and resources. Instead, they look for ways to save money, maximize time, and protect resources.

In project management, this is called the triple constraint—time, scope, and cost.

**TIME:** How much time is the training going to take to deliver?

How much time will be lost from the employees while being trained?

**SCOPE:** What is the scope of the training?

What should it include and not include?

Did it meet the expected outcomes?

**COST:** How much will this training cost, including travel,

time away from work, meals, etc.?

Will the benefit outweigh the cost?

*The triple constraint collectively restricts what can be accomplished with the training, but it can also be thoughtfully approached.* As the trainer, you can be intentional with how the time is spent to maximize moments, what the scope includes to broaden results, and how to minimize costs by making sure every moment counts.

Maximizing moments involves a carefully planned schedule for the day that includes brain breaks and opportunities to process the information being shared. In the structure chapter, there are specific ways to build the structure of the day effectively to maximize learning.

Specifically, designing what will be taught during training will help focus all energy and effort towards those specific outcomes. In the section on clarity I share strategies that help determine how to write objectives that will focus the attention of the learning opportunity on the topics needed for learning.

Cost is always a concern when conducting a training session. Carefully planned training will increase the opportunity for learning during the training and improve accountability for the new information after the training. That combination will enhance the return on investment for the organization and increase your value to the company.

Professional learning, if not done well, can be an expensive timewaster, and can lead to missed deadlines and frustrated employers, employees, and customers. We teach people things hoping they learn and in turn improve job performance, efficiency, and effectiveness. The goal of training is to advance systems, sometimes by changing practice. When learning does not stick, re-training must happen, perpetuating a negative cycle. Improving the return on investment from professional learning can improve end results while saving money, time and resources. Why wouldn't all organizations want this outcome?

Intentional objectives, solid teaching practices and follow-up opportunities for learning will increase an organization's return on investment from professional learning. The adults must be taught, refreshed, retrained, or enhanced to retain and utilize what they are learning.

Improving professional learning practices allows for people to feel successful at their jobs. They feel better equipped to do the work in a way that is effective and efficient. It's about the facilitator and the leadership teams seeing the whole person, who wants to be the best he or she can but needs support to do so. ***It is not about seeing your employees as tools who need to be sharpened.*** Job satisfaction improves when employees feel they are being equipped to do the job well. That does not mean your professional learning opportunities are automatically beneficial, however. Your training must be crafted to meet the needs of the participants while building skills for successful implementation.

According to the Association for Talent Development, if a company offers a comprehensive training program, they have 218% higher income per employee than companies with no formal training. These companies also have a 24% higher profit margin than those who spend less on training. ***Employee productivity increases when training is effective and relevant.***

Overwhelmingly, employees want to do well in their jobs. In fact, 40% of employees who do not receive the necessary training to do their jobs well will leave their positions within the first year. In a study of 400 employees from three generations, 70% said job-related development opportunities influenced them to stay in their jobs.

These statistics matter because engaged employees outperform by 202% those who are disengaged. That is a large enough percentage to turn heads.

Middlesex University for Work Based Learning interviewed 4,300 employees. Of those, 74% said they were not achieving their full potential at work because they did not have the appropriate training and development opportunities. How are those appropriate training and development opportunities created? Your training can equip participants to feel more competent in their jobs.

## PERFORMANCE VS. LEARNING ZONE:

I cannot type the phrase "let me know" without messing it up. I took typing in high school from the same old-school secretary who also taught shorthand. We learned on typewriters with correction tabs and sat up straight or caught a ruler to our knuckles. I am a proficient typist, except when typing this three-word phrase.

The sad part is that I probably type this phrase five times a day. Why am I not any better at it? Because I do not ever put myself in the learning zone and practice it. If I spent five minutes practicing typing…let me know, let me know, let me know…over and over again, I would improve. Instead of doing that, though, I leave myself in the performance zone and only type the phrase when it matters.

The intent of professional development is to improve procedure. Employees must feel safe to practice new learning. Once employees learn a new way of work, they must feel safe to put it into practice. One of the best ways to help people feel safe with new information, is to allow them to practice it in a supportive, low-stakes environment.

Low-stakes environments called "Learning Zones" are created specifically for practice and learning, giving employees space to make mistakes without significant cost. You can practice the new sales technique with other salespeople rather than with a potential customer. You can rehearse a new type of surgical stitch in a skills lab rather than on an actual patient. You can explore how to use the register before you have actual customers.

Eduardo Briceno delivers an excellent Ted Talk about the performance zone vs. the learning zone. In it, he describes the performance zone as a space where you must execute flawlessly, and failure is costly. An excellent example of the performance zone would be when a surgeon is performing knee surgery. As the patient, I need my surgeon to be in the performance zone during my surgery. My full recovery is about as high stakes as it gets. But I also need him to have spent significant time in the learning zone, where mistakes are expected and encouraged; and failure is part of the learning process.

Training or professional learning is the perfect time to be in the learning zone, and participants must know the mistakes they make are acceptable and encouraged. That is part of your role as the facilitator to make the learning zone a safe place.

Participants may be from the same organization or field of expertise. This could create a potentially competitive environment, where participants are hesitant to show they are in the learning zone. As the facilitator, you must make it safe for the learning to happen. Throughout this book, we will talk through ways to make it safe for the learners and ways to create a learning zone environment for every participant.

When does "learning zone" learning happen?

What if it could at least start during a training session?

How might learning zone learning increase a willingness to try new things?

When in a professional learning session, what if participants were given the opportunity to practice the new skills with one another, without the threat of failure?

Let me know, let me know, let me know, let me know.

## IMPROVE MORALE

People feel more confident when equipped to do their jobs well. One of my business colleagues shared his need to create teamwork with his training. He wants his team to rely on one another for success. As a trainer, you can create opportunities for this type of collaboration to carry over into daily work as well. In the Make Learning Logical chapter, you will find specific strategies that build space for this to happen.

Safety comes with numbers. If I am supported in my learning and can do it with others, I will take risks.

In addition to teamwork, a great training experience equips people with new skills for doing their jobs. As I said before, one wakes up in the morning and says, "I want to be terrible at my job today." And yet, some people are currently terrible at their jobs. They do not have the tools to be great yet. Effective training experiences can create space for employees to gain the tools and skills needed to be great. You, as the facilitator, will usher them into that type of learning space, and walk through the learning with them as their guide.

## EVOKE CHANGE

Often professional learning opportunities are brought in to create change in the organization. It might be to improve a system or to approach clients differently. There are many reasons why organizations invest in training, but most of the time it is because something needs to change.

There are two problems to overcome here: fear of change and lack of connection to the work.

Many people find change difficult. ***The number one error organizations make when trying to evoke change is allowing too much complacency.*** It is mission-critical to create a high sense of urgency in fellow managers and employees, that this is a change worth making.

People learn by doing something, not by listening to people tell them how to do something. There must be connections to the work as well as job-embedded opportunities to practice the shift.

In Michael Fullan's book, *The Six Secrets of Change*, secret four is Learning is the Work. He emphasizes the need to embed the learning into the work of the employees. It is not wise to only practice outside of the work environment. If you want change to stick, you give people space to try out the new knowledge in their workspace.

If you wish to improve job performance, you identify critical knowledge, transfer this knowledge using job instruction, and verify learning and success.

Make it clear learning needs to stick for improved job satisfaction as well as productivity. Knowing is half the battle. Doing something about it is what will create new opportunities and ultimately change.

***The knowing/doing gap is difficult for anyone to overcome.*** Knowing something needs to be done differently is the first step in instituting change. Acting on that need for change is the second step, but the space between the two can be gigantic.

Throughout this book, beginning with Make Learning Safe, I will share tried and true ways to engage adult learners and tap into their innate desire to learn. Tapping into the desire to learn will help make the learning stick, leading to a change in practice. My goal is to shrink the space between step one and step two, so you can easily progress from knowing to doing.

The "Knowing/Doing Gap" describes when knowing how to do something does not necessarily translate into doing that something. Often, we get stuck between knowing something should be done a certain way and doing it the way it should be done. You want participants to know the information and be able to do something with the learning.

### How can you ensure that "doing" happens?

Being brilliant at the content is where many people excel. You know everything that needs to be said and could do it backwards and forwards. You can sing every word to "The Devil Went Down to Georgia" in the shower and nail every word. The problem is, when you have a microphone in your hand and an audience in front of you, you stop having fun with it and you start reading the words you already know, not trusting yourself to get it right. Let loose a little and trust the brilliance you have. The goal is for others to know it like you do, and reading to them will not make that a reality.

# NEED TO KNOW

Focus on the adult learner and the why of learning, giving purpose to the training experience.

Know why it is valuable to make learning safe, logical, fun, and memorable.

Spend significant time in the learning zone when facilitating a learning experience.

# NOTE-TAKING

Embrace and evoke change.

What are two ideas from this chapter that have piqued your interest?

What additional information do you hope to gain about these topics?

What do you need to do to incorporate these ideas into your work with adult learners?

# NEXT STEPS

How will you ensure you sound great the next time you sing karaoke?

For more ideas and explanations around adult learning or reasons why learning should stick, visit www.learningcanstick.com

# Make Learning Safe

Music, the kind that makes you tap your toe and remember your high school prom, is playing. When you walk in, I greet you at the door with a sticker and a smile. You are immediately introduced to a new person and learn something about that person that relates to you, too. The tables are round and set up for collaboration, and there is candy in the middle of every single one.

You just walked into my training room. For well over a decade I have created this atmosphere for my participants. It does not matter if I have 10 people or 100, the feeling is the same. You belong here and you are safe with me.

I will know your name within the first hour and will make sure I use it every time we speak. In fact, I will manage to say your name at least three times within the first five minutes of knowing you. More importantly, you will know the names of the other people at your table, even if you did not know them before you came.

The objectives for our time together will be clearly displayed and will relate directly back to what you do every day.

My room is always safe and primed for learning and growth.

To learn anything, humans have an innate need to feel safe in the learning space. I mentioned the learning zone in the last chapter, which is the space where it is possible to grow and absorb new information. The learning zone is only productive when the stakes are low. The number one rule for the learning zone is to make it safe.

The safety in this case is emotional and psychological. Emotional safety allows for the learner to feel supported, not judged. Building relationships with the learner is paramount to having a successful learning session.

As a facilitator of learning, you must genuinely desire to get to know your participants, whether you see them daily, weekly, or once in a lifetime. You must legitimately want to usher them into the learning zone with your learning opportunity. And there must be validity to your skills and understanding of the content.

Don't try to be Mariah Carey, but instead pick a song everyone can comfortably sing.

# *Clarity*

## MAKES LEARNING STICK

# NEED TO KNOW

- Determine the what and how to your why

- Make the why clear

- Let the participants wrestle with the purpose

Adult learners need to know why they are learning what is being taught. The why is the hook. The catch. The reason for putting in effort. Without the why, learning will be spotty at best and will not likely stick. Your why must be clear.

**Facilitator:** Welcome. I will be your trainer today. This is going to be a day full of learning. Here we go…six hours later the trainer is still talking, and you have yet to figure out why you attended this training. The trainer never asked you what you, as the learner, needed or how the material connected to your work. You completed the hours, but you left without a plan or a desire to utilize what you experienced during the training in your work.

*Has this ever happened to you?*

As a facilitator, your role is to make the learning applicable and engaging so the learning sticks. Over the next chapters, we will explore training strategies to increase your tools to make that happen. Let's get better together.

## BEGIN WITH CLARITY OF PURPOSE

Learning about something that is relevant and useful will stick more than something obscure and non-applicable. Great trainers make the why abundantly clear.

During a recent project management training I learned a phrase from Dr. Brene Brown that will forever change my approach to, well, almost everything.

*"Clear is kind."*

Our church built a chapel a couple years ago, and my husband and I serve as marriage mentors for that chapel. Every couple getting married in the chapel must go through four mentoring sessions prior to their wedding. We use our 21 years of marriage as a road map to equip these couples with the tools they need to fight fair and love completely.

The number one tool we give to our couples is "Clear is kind." In a marriage, the spouse can never read the other person's mind. No amount of time together allows that to happen. Instead, spouses need to be clear with their needs, expectations, desires, and wants if they ever wish to have those needs met.

This concept translates directly into training scenarios.

When working with others, the clearer you are with your expectations and your outcomes, the more likely you are to get the intended results. They cannot read your mind any more than your spouse can.

Often, when conducting a professional development opportunity, it is taken for granted the participants know why they are there and what they should learn. As facilitators of high-quality professional learning, we cannot assume participants know why they are at your training, or what they should gain from attending. Instead, we must take the time to make the purpose crystal clear.

## TWO TYPES OF TRAINING OBJECTIVES:

Ultimately, objectives are the "need to know" and "how you will learn" portions of your training. Clarity of purpose requires communication to participants around two types of training objectives—performance objectives and learning objectives.

A performance objective captures what the participants should know and be able to do at the end of the training. Learning objectives are the specific way or ways participants are going to engage in the learning during the training to reach the performance objectives.

Here are a few examples.

| Performance Objective: | Learning Objective: |
|---|---|
| **What you are going to be able to accomplish as a result of the training?** | **How you are going to reach your performance objectives during the training?** |
| Be able to create reports using Access | Engage in practice using Access to create reports |
| Perform CPR when needed | Roleplay CPR using a dummy |
| Successfully navigate the new operating system to improve efficiency | Work through scenarios using the new operating system |

If you are clear with the desired performance and learning objectives, participants will see a cohesive flow of learning and a focus and clarity about their training experience. In this book, I will call learning objectives, "need to know" items; and you will find them at the beginning and end of each chapter. As you read, they should help bring clarity to your learning.

Creating these objectives should be a team effort. Talk with the leadership team of the organization to determine what they want the training to accomplish. If you work for a different organization and are helping train on a product or service, share your objectives with the leadership team ahead of time to ensure you are meeting their needs. You might have a very clear idea of what you are going to teach; but if it isn't what they thought they were going to receive, they are not going to feel it was successfully accomplished.

Once you create objectives, designing the training will become much more aligned. Now, instead of a random collection of activities, you will have a cohesive flow of learning which ends with the desired outcomes. This brings focus and clarity to the training.

Objectives are just as important when conducting a meeting with your staff or having a conversation with your teenage son. Objectives are the road map to learning.

When I am going to talk with my 19-year-old son about school, I have objectives for the conversation. I could go in multiple directions.

*"Son, I am so proud of how hard you are working in that class."*
(Objective: Build him up to keep working hard.)

*"Son, I do not understand how you missed classes this week when I know you had absolutely nothing else to do."*
(Objective: Shame him into doing better.)

*"Son, I know you are capable of so many awesome things. I can't wait for you to impress me with your grades at the end of the term."*
(Objective: Pressure him into working hard when he might not have been.)

Mothers are masterful at navigating the roadmap of getting what they need or want out of a conversation. Trainers need to be equally masterful.

This navigation to the right destination will only work if the trainer, manager, teacher, or boss knows where she is headed in the long run.

Participants are more likely to buy in if they understand why they are asked to do something. In preparation for this book I interviewed education and business leaders about their struggles when offering training. Buy-in, open mindedness and willingness to learn were the top three answers from business and educational leaders when asked about their challenges with trainings. You must be upfront with the participants on the value of their attending this training. Help them see from the beginning to the end how they will use the information they are learning.

## HOW TO MAKE THE WHY CLEAR

If you are clear with the "why" behind the training being conducted, the participants will determine for themselves the value and importance of what you are sharing with them. Keep the "why" of the learning front and center for every participant.

Simon Sinek's Golden Circle from his book, *Start with Why?* explains the value and importance of making the why the focus and the first action in any situation.

Sinek says, "People don't buy what you do; they buy why you do it." This statement absolutely rings true in professional learning.

In training, we must make the why personal and clear for participants, so they see the value in participating. One way to do that involves communicating clear and specific objectives around the intended outcomes of the training and how the participants will engage in the learning.

When you are clear with your objectives for a training, the participants will be more likely to embrace and understand the key information. Without clear objectives, you are going on a journey without a destination. That might be fun when you get to pick the adventure; but when a professional learning opportunity is involved, if you clearly articulate the purpose of the training, and the goals accomplished during the training, the guesswork disappears and is replaced by clarity and focus.

During the training, as early as possible, state the objectives and make sure the participants can relate to and understand them. There are many strategies for engaging participants in connecting with the training objectives.

**Avoid just telling the participants the objectives.** Instead let them talk about the objectives. Let them wrestle with the reasons behind the objectives. This conversation does not need to be lengthy, five minutes at the most, but the impact will be permanent.

Have participants read the objectives out loud as a choral read and discuss them as a table group or in partners. Provide stem questions such as:

- Which objective are you most excited to accomplish?
- Which objective relates most directly to your work?
- How will work productivity improve if the objective is met?

**Post the objectives somewhere they can be seen and revisited all day.** If you don't want to leave them posted, then have them as part of your slide deck at the beginning, middle and end of your training so participants can see where they are heading and the progress they are making to get to that destination.

By asking the participants to share what they are thinking about the objectives, they are making connections and internalizing the information,

making it their own. As you will hear in upcoming chapters, the more you let the participants do the talking, the more they will learn.

As mentioned previously, when making learning stick, participants must be able to relate to what they are learning. The more they interact with the information the more likely it will become what they know.

- What do I want people to be able to do after this training?
- What strategies or activities will I use to ensure the desired learning takes place?
- Who needs to be involved to make this type of learning happen?

# NEED TO KNOW

Determine the what and how of your why by creating performance and learning objectives that are revisited throughout the training.

Make the why clear by guiding the learners to determine the why themselves.

Let the participants wrestle with the purpose behind the training.

# NOTE-TAKING

Write down one or two ideas you can use based on your reading in this chapter. What do you need to know or do to make this work in your training sessions?

# NEXT STEPS

Every one of us has a different note-taking style. Some of us were taught how, but most of us just figured out somewhere along the way what worked for us. Throughout this book, I am going to encourage that you take some notes. Those might be done in the margins as you read, or maybe on a separate notebook, either analog or digital. That is what notes are designed to do. They help you process your learning.

# Authenticity

### MAKES LEARNING STICK

## NEED TO KNOW

- Make connections with people and for people.

- Be your authentic self.

- Be a winner and avoid your inner whiner and wiener tendencies.

- Mix it up for the participants.

- Trust the learning is happening.

You, as the facilitator, have made it clear this learning is relevant to the learner. Now you need to let the participants know you have the credibility necessary to make the learning stick.

*Welcome. Are you here for my party? This is going to be an epic day of learning! Since you are here early, I need your help. As people come in, can you please help them get all the materials they need for success today? If people come to your table, can you welcome them? Tell me something memorable about you.*

I have been described as a bold flavor. When I am on, I am ON. My father is an entertainer by profession; therefore I grew up knowing how to be on stage and capture an audience's attention. There is a persona that kicks in when I have an audience, but that persona is just an amped-up version of who I am every single day. I genuinely want to know more about who you are and what makes you tick. I am truly passionate about learning, and that translates into my daily actions. I want to hear about your favorite sports team or where you had dinner last night. I care about you.

This might not be true for you, but there are portions of your personality you can play up in a training setting that will make your audience trust you from the beginning. It happens in the first two minutes of your time with them and lasts for a lifetime.

*How do you build trust? Authenticity. You must be willing to be yourself and let the best parts of your personality shine through.*

Authenticity is one of the most valuable things you can carry with you into a training. People will pick up on a disingenuous nature immediately, if not sooner. You must be an amped up version of yourself, however, if you want to engage your audience.

Entertainment is the action of providing or being provided with amusement or enjoyment. Learning needs to be a form of entertainment to stick. That entertainment needs to be relevant and real, however, which is where authenticity comes into play.

My children claim that I have a phone voice and a stage voice. I suppose that is true. When I am on the phone, I am demanding someone's attention and I need to change the way I speak to do that. My stage voice, well, that is a different situation all together.

It is almost like a switch. I turn it on when it is time to capture attention. It can happen at a dinner party, social event, or a training situation. When the switch is on all my senses are heightened and I am working the room. I am making connections with the people around me, and in turn connecting the people in the room with one another.

What flips your switch? When are you the most "on?" Does that translate into a training situation? Why or why not?

WRITE YOUR THOUGHTS HERE:

# MAKE CONNECTIONS

Make sure you have had a conversation with every single participant that enters your room within the first five minutes of the training. This could be a simple handshake and hello, or it could be a question and answer session going over the needs for the day. It works well to learn something about each person right away. Ask a question about an item they are wearing or carrying that will tell you something about their personality. Learn about the people with whom you are interacting.

**Instant connections.** Who is your audience? What do you have in common with them? What will make you credible with them? How can you get that information into the room right away?

I carry a YETI cup with a Florida State University and University of North Florida sticker on it. Each sticker represents my kids' colleges, but they also serve as a great conversation starter. I have often gotten a "Go Noles" or a "Swoop" as an instant greeting before I ever said anything.

Something this simple makes you human. You need the learner to see you as approachable and authentic. By sharing that I have children, I become a real, live person instead of some person sent here to teach something.

Notice things about your participants to help you connect and remember them. Look for defining characteristics, and I do not necessarily mean looks.

Do they have a logo on their shirt?

Do they like a certain type of drink?

Is there a sticker on their computer signifying an alma mater or allegiance to Marvel or Star Wars?

Is she wearing Minnie Mouse earrings?

Are you from the same state?

Do you like the same music?

How can you connect? Ask questions to learn more. These instant connections can last for days, weeks or even years.

First impressions are everything. In fact, according to the book *Captivate*, first and final impressions are decided in the first two seconds of seeing someone. Even after you spend a substantial amount of time with that same person, your original opinion of that person rarely changes. Instead, those first two seconds must be done well.

When people enter your training space, they form an opinion of you in exactly two seconds! That opinion shapes their desire to learn from you as well. No pressure or anything.

They are looking at your eyes, smile, and hands. You must connect with them immediately and can do so by simply greeting them at the door. Make full eye contact and introduce yourself to each person as he or she makes his/her way into the room. These are your people, so make sure they know that right away. Your level of enthusiasm will be contagious, so give them something worth catching.

It is your job to create an instant atmosphere where learning is safe and fun. This sounds easy, and, quite honestly, it is. You just help people see you are authentically invested in their learning and growth.

When you enter my space, you will be greeted with a sticker and a smile. I will likely run halfway around the room to give you said sticker, and I will be sure to look you straight in the eye. I will break the silence, so you do not have to do so. If we are one on one, I will carry the conversation as best I can, but I will not dominate the conversation. In other words, I will make it my mission to make you feel at ease.

Your audience is determining right away if you are a winner or a loser. I know you are a winner, but how will you make sure they do also? Carry

 yourself with confidence. Hold your head high. Do not fidget or look down. Shoulders back, chin up, eyes forward. Winners do not look at their feet; they look at their audiences.

I have a friend who tends to be very introspective. Recently, he had a conversation with his team about the types of people they hoped to be. They discussed being *winners, whiners,* or *wieners.* I laughed when he first told me, but then we dug deeper; and he was spot on with his assessment. He was working on his response to different circumstances.

There is one other type of person…the wino, but that is another story for another day.

He said sometimes he responds like a wiener, wishy washy and unsure of what he should do in that situation. Other times he is a whiner, fussing about what could have been or what should be instead of embracing what is. His goal is to be a winner. A winner responds with a positive attitude and approach to all circumstances.

As a trainer, you need to have a winner's response. Your participants will follow your lead. If the projector will not work, instead of whining, grab some chart paper and recreate your first slide while you have the room work on creating name tents and getting to know one another; then call someone to fix the projector. If it is hot in the room, send the group on a walk and talk and let the participants get some fresh air while you call maintenance. Winners find solutions. Be a winner.

What can you do to avoid being a whiner or a wiener, and instead be a winner? (with your staff, patient, spouse, participants, students)

WRITE YOUR THOUGHTS HERE:

# BE REAL

Have you ever gone to a multi-day training and not learned the names of anyone else there, including the trainer?

Have you ever wondered why the trainer was qualified to teach you, because he or she didn't take the time to become credible?

Have you ever traveled more than 50 miles to attend a training that could have been accomplished via email, because there was no human interaction?

When working for a district as an educational leader, I was selected to be a part of a turn-around leadership program. Ten of us were selected to be trained to be principals of schools in need, and we worked together once a month for over a year. About three months into the project we went to Miami for a training that included all the districts in the state that were participating in this program. We arrived on a Wednesday and went to dinner as a team. We all talked about how excited we were to work with people from other parts of the state to see what sort of innovation was happening elsewhere.

We walked into the training room the next morning, and like any good team, commandeered a table so we could all sit together. Teams are often like pack animals. The business department sits together. Accounting sits separately from sales. Teams stick together. The training started at 8:00 am and lasted until 5:00 pm. Not once in those nine hours did we talk to anyone other than our table group. I held out hope day two would look different. Guess what, it did not. On our way home on Friday, I realized we could have gotten just as much out of the training virtually, in our county, with the ten people in our cohort. There was so much brilliance in the room, and we didn't get to experience any of it.

The trainer didn't bother to introduce himself to us nor let us introduce ourselves to one another. We sat and listened, with little time to process or participate. I would like to think this type of training is rare, but I know better. Often, the trainer is perceived to hold all the information, that information is delivered to the participants, the end.

Maybe you have inadvertently conducted a training that fits this description. Never again.

There is an incredible amount of brain power in any room of participants. Capitalize on it.

Being real with your participants means you give them a voice, and you listen when that voice speaks. Yes, you as the trainer are the one with the information right now, but they are the ones who must implement the information in their daily work. They need to be the ones to digest the information; and for that to happen, they must feel safe to learn.

It is just as imperative you are real in a one-on-one setting as it is in a large-group setting. If you are training someone in your office, you need to help that person see the real you right away. You also need to take the time to get to know him or her too. Ask questions and listen to the answers. Offer up information about who you are so the person knows you are worth hearing. If you are working one on one with a patient, let the person know she matters to you; and you are listening.

Being real also means letting the participants know why you are the best man or woman for the job of teaching this content. Let them know your background, your relevant experiences, and your credibility for this role. The relevance of those factors will be specific to the content you are presenting to a particular audience. Maybe you used to be a nurse and you now work to train first-year nurses. They need to know you have been in their shoes. Maybe you work for Salesforce. They need to know you used to be a customer prior to becoming part of the sales and training team.

In my career, I have been a science teacher, elective teacher, youth pastor, curriculum designer, assistant principal, district director, academic coach, tutor, volunteer, project systems coach, program manager, division liaison, program specialist, and associate area director. If I stood up in front of a group of participants in a training and rattled off that list of job titles, I would just look pompous or arrogant. I, instead, need to share only the experiences that are relevant to the training at hand.

Let's pretend I am training a team of trainers who work for the Human

Resources team of a pharmaceutical company. I am there to teach them how to get learning to stick. My introduction would sound something like this.

*Welcome to our training today. My name is Dr. Christie McMullen and I am here in the name of good teaching. I have spent the last twenty-one years in the educational field, but for the last 14 years I have specifically trained adults. Although I have served in a multitude of roles over my tenure the one most relevant to you and what we are going to do today is my most recent role of Associate Area Director. It is my job to sell our product in four states and make sure implementation of that product is well received by the partners purchasing it and well managed by our team members assigned to support the implementation of it. My goal today is to use the experience I have in getting adults to learn to help you have added success when you are working with your team to roll out new products and services. Let's get started.*

I did not give a laundry list of jobs I had done, but I did let them know I had established myself in my field. I threw in "Dr.," even though that still makes me a little uncomfortable, because mentioning my title shows I have mastered my content. I mentioned the role that was most relevant to my audience, and I established credibility for sharing my ideas with the team.

Take a moment to write out your introduction for a specific audience. Pick one relevant to you.

Teaching and learning start the moment participants arrive, and they do not stop until months or even years later, if done right. The minute people arrive you are setting the tone for a positive learning experience. You get to set the stage, and it is valuable you pay attention to the little things. Help them be comfortable and make yourself credible. Once those two things have happened you can start working on the content you were hired to teach.

Here are a few ways to create a safe and productive learning space without adding any time to your training.

It is just as important you are real with your staff members daily as it is that you are real with a room full of strangers.

You need to be your most authentic self in every circumstance and create space for people to learn from one another in all situations, not just training room ones.

This might look like you, as the boss, admitting when you do not understand something. Or it might mean offering time in the day for people to practice a new technique without judgment or pressure. Being real means allowing people to see the authenticity in you and one another.

### USE MUSIC

Music can be the great equalizer. There is extensive research on the number of beats per minute and what each speed evokes in people. In my experience though, classics work every time. Throw in some Michael Jackson, Madonna, and Prince, with a splash of rock and a clean rap song or two and people from all walks of life will relax almost instantly. Music breaks the ice while you are getting set up and sets the mood for the rest of the day.

Make sure the music is already playing when the participants arrive. It should not be so loud people cannot talk over it, but it should be loud enough to make conversation safe. It is hard to talk to strangers in a completely silent room. A little bit of music breaks down barriers. And a great playlist can get a roomful of strangers to become instant friends. I have had people cha cha slide an hour into training. Be brave.

> Want some great, tried and true playlists? Visit: LearningCanStick.com

I will get more specific about music in the Make Learning Fun chapter.

### INTRODUCE PEOPLE TO ONE ANOTHER AT THE DOOR

When someone enters the room, shake his/her hand and introduce yourself. Duh. Except, when you do, repeat the name out loud, then connect him to another learner.

*"Hi Jackson, my name is Christie. Jackson, what brings you to this training today, besides your boss? Jackson, could I ask you to be in charge of your table and make sure everyone completes the task on the board. Jackson, that lady over there is named Jackie. Why don't you sit with her? You can be my "Jack-of-all-trades" table.*

Corny? A little. Productive? Absolutely. The act of repeating the names as you learn them burns them into your brain and shows them you value their presence. ***It is much more difficult to disappear after a break if the trainer knows your name.***

This takes practice, but I assure you, it works. I have learned 80+ names on day one of a three-day training in the first 20 minutes of the day using this technique. You do not have to have a great memory, just strong technique.

When you are working one on one with someone, learning his/her name is considerably easier than when it is a large group. That said, it is no less significant. Call the person by name often to make him/her feel seen. We all like to hear our name spoken. We appreciate someone taking the time to learn our name and pronounce it correctly. Do not abbreviate it or change it just because it is difficult to pronounce or hard for you to remember. If you are going to write it down somewhere, double check the spelling. This shows you are paying attention to the person specifically and not making assumptions.

> Want to see this technique in action? Visit: LearningCanStick.com

## USE NAMES TO MAKE INSTANT CONNECTIONS

Name tags help but kick it up a notch. Ask the participants to write something unusual about themselves on the nametags to help you remember them. This is a great conversation starter between participants as well as with you and the participants.

— Conversation Starters —

Favorite vacation spot
Most embarrassing moment
Years in the business
Something important to you
Favorite hobby
Desired outcome of the training
Draw your family
Picture of your favorite pastime
Something that makes you laugh

Here are a few examples of conversation starters that can be written or even drawn in the corners of the name tag. Or, you can also have the participants make a name tent. This is just a folded piece of cardstock the participants personalize. Have them write their name largely in the middle and put their answers to some of these prompts in the corners.

Having an example is a helpful tool to show what your expectations might be.

Once participants create personalized name tents or tags, allow them to share with others what they created. This can be done as a table group or as an entire room. Encourage participants to introduce themselves to five people in the room, using their name tag as a guide. This increases relational capacity and boosts morale. Now the participants don't matter just to you, but to one another as well.

If you have more than 15 people, I do not recommend each person share his/her unique quality with the entire group. People have a short attention span and will zone out as people do their introductions. "Mix it up" has some suggestions for how to get people to introduce themselves in a large setting and not lose interest.

## MIX IT UP

People naturally gravitate towards their comfort zone. If people are reluctant to initially sit with people they do not know, just wait and change it up during the training. Encourage people to sit with colleagues from different departments/divisions. This may take some prodding and does not necessarily need to happen at the beginning of the training, but it does need to happen at some point.

Since it is difficult to get people to start the day out of their comfort zones, let them sit where they wish, then move people around more than once during the training. This spreads the brilliance in the room. Ask them to share something they heard with a partner from another table. Regroup them according to a random factor, like shirt color or gender. You can get creative with this type of regrouping. Hair color, eye color, height, years with the company, distance traveled to get to the training, birthday and so on. Some are easy to spot (shirt color) and others require interaction (birthday), but all are effective.

Activities like this force people to step outside their departments, their friends, their comfort zones, and learn from others. People have so much to give one another; but we, as trainers, have to create space for giving to take please.

Allow people chances to talk to one another. Miami was not the only training I attended with people from all over the country, and didn't actually interact with anyone but my table group. Unfortunately, I came to the training with most of my tablemates and could have talked to them back at my office. Does that sound familiar?

Here another way to get people rearranged:

Play music and ask participants to move around the room, saying hello to those around them. When the music stops, call out a number, (i.e. 4) and ask participants to get into a group with that many people total. For safe, easy conversation, larger groups work well. When you want them to discuss content or a sensitive subject, call out 2 or 3 as a group number so everyone can share safely.

This activity can be used to break the ice at the beginning of the training or later in the training to share important content. I have included a few suggested questions below.

| Large Group Questions: | Small Group Questions: |
|---|---|
| Where do you like to vacation? | What is your biggest fear? |
| What is one take away from the last hour of discussion? | How are you going to use what we learned in the last hour in your daily work? |
| Describe your job in 3 words. | Describe your job in 30 seconds. |
| What is your favorite color? | Describe your work as a color and explain why. |
| What is one thing you have learned in the last 30 minutes? | How will you apply one thing you have learned in the last 30 minutes? |

## GIVE AND TAKE INFORMATION

Another great way to get people to talk to a new group is to give and take information. In this activity you write down a new learning, idea or understanding on a post-it note. Writing down the idea is the first step towards memorizing the information. Having something written down also makes this activity feel safer, because if I draw a blank, I have a written reminder of what I was going to say. Remember this is new learning, so the safer you can make it, the better.

When the music starts, move around the room, dancing if they wish. When the music stops, find a partner, share your idea and have him/her share his/her idea. Swap post-it notes. Start the music and this time when it stops, share the new idea instead of your own.

The give and take information can be the topic you most recently discussed, or it can be a review of something that happened earlier in the day or the day before. By discussing the learning with other people in the room, participants are able to solidify ideas and understanding.

Allow these conversations to happen multiple times throughout the day. In this version, participants would actually take the post-it note from the other person so that the other person's understanding or learning now becomes their own. You could also let them keep their own information and share it multiple times with multiple partners.

## ACKNOWLEDGE THE OBVIOUS

The brilliance is found in the people in the room, not in the trainer. Honor that brilliance by letting their voices be heard.

After delivering a chunk of the learning material in a professional learning setting, allow the participants to talk about it. Give them a prompt, a specific amount of time, then let them go. "We just learned about the importance of our new marketing plan; please talk with a partner about how this new plan will impact your daily work. You will have 5 minutes to talk with your partner." And the screen says, "How will this new marketing plan affect your daily work?" or "What are three ways you can use this new system when supporting clients?"

At the end of the five minutes ask for one or two volunteers from different departments to share their understanding of how this new system will impact the daily work. This will put several perspectives in the room, from the people who are going to be doing the work. Of course, you as the trainer could predict how the learning will be used, but it is much more powerful if the participants figure that out for themselves.

If there is a notion the training is going to be redundant or painful, call it like it is; then surprise them.


My husband and I have best friends who have both been physical therapists for over twenty years. Every two years they are required to take CPR as a continuing education opportunity. They know the concepts of CPR like the back of their hands and Staying Alive is still the song used to teach the rhythm. This is not new information, nor is this course particularly enlightening for them. They could easily teach this course, and yet, they have to take it every three years.

As the trainer, call out that obvious fact in the room.

*"Please stand if you have taken a CPR class before. Stay standing if you have done it more than three times. Stay standing if you have taken it more than five times. Remain standing if you have taken it more than 10 times. Ladies and gentlemen, look around; these are your experts. Talk as a table group about a time you used CPR to save a life. What aspects of the process did you underestimate? What missing components of the practical aspects of CPR need to be addressed today?"*

Throughout the training, use those experts. Honor what they know and use that knowledge to shape the learning for the day. How different would the experience be if you no longer assumed you were alone in knowing the content?

## HONOR THE BRILLIANCE IN THE ROOM

Almost always, someone in the room knows something about the topic at hand. Do not ignore that knowledge. Celebrate it. Here are a couple easy ways to recognize the group for what they know while building credibility for you.

Ask collectively how many years of experience in this business or on this topic exist in the group, like the PT example above. Let each table add up their years and write them on chart paper at the front. Use that total as a wow factor for the learning that can take place based on the expertise.

Honor expertise by letting people brainstorm before giving answers.

Before sharing a concept, let people talk about what they know about the concept. Use what they know to your advantage. Do not just ignore the newfound knowledge and feel you must cover the known topics in redundancy. Instead let people share what they know with one another; then let them ask what they still need to know.

A great way to do this is through a simple activity.

Pair people who have a strong understanding of a topic with those who are novices. Ask people to line up according to how much they feel they know about a topic. A one lines up at the far left and feels he does not know anything about the subject being covered. A ten feels he or she could teach the topic, and he lines up on the far right. You line up wherever you feel you are on the continuum. Once everyone is in place, you simply fold the line in half, partnering the ones with the tens and so forth in between. Then allow the partners to share with one another what they know and understand about the topic. Once they have had a chance to share, have them go back to their tables and talk about what they learned. Then ask what they still need to know; and that, my friends, is what you will cover in your session.

Use table experts whenever possible.

If you are saying something the participants can say/learn/discover for themselves, stop and let them do the talking. When you find yourself saying something they could easily read and understood, let them read. If you are repeating something the participants could repeat, let them. The person doing the talking is the person doing the learning, remember? Let them do the talking.

This may require asking some questions in the beginning to determine who knows what at the tables. You may also want to rearrange participants to ensure the experts are spread around the room. Experts are not always the most seasoned veterans but instead those who have been voracious learners. Let the table experts lead the conversation at the tables around your topics. This will give people a chance to hear from one another and not just you.

## TRUST THE LEARNING IS HAPPENING

You do not have to be the one to say something for it to be learned. If you give participants the information and ask them to wrestle with it, read it, discuss it, and learn it, they will. Build the structure for learning then let them go. Part of being authentic is recognizing the participants are the ones doing this work every day. They need to go back to their jobs with the knowledge and understanding of the content. As the trainer, you must let them learn and guide them in the process.

The biggest concern trainers have with letting go of the control of the content is not knowing if the participants are learning the information. Formative assessments are an excellent way to determine if the learning is successful.

Formative assessments can be used to check in with the audience throughout the day to ensure the key points have been covered. Formative assessments are tasks that allow you to know what the participants know and understand at that point in the training. This can be done in a variety of ways. Maybe you use a few questions you want to be sure the participants can answer.

This does not need to be a sophisticated process. My favorite formative assessment is a post-it note during break that goes on a poster on the way out of the room. Ask for one thing they have learned so far today to be put on one note and one thing they want or need to know more about on the other. Place them on the poster in the back. During break, you can read those notes and determine what stuck and what needs to be covered again. This information will inform and help form your next steps as a trainer, hence formative assessments.

> **Want some great polling options? Visit: LearningCanStick.com**

There are some great apps that help make the sharing of answers fun and informative for you. You will know immediately if the participants got the answers right, helping you decide what needs to be covered again. Right now, in 2020 a few fun ones include Kahoot, Padlet, Plickers, and Poll Anywhere.

# NEED TO KNOW

Make connections with people and for people. Find ways to learn who they are right away and use those connections to keep the participants engaged and interested.

Be your authentic self, while finding ways to capture your audience.

Be a winner and avoid your inner whiner and wiener tendencies.

Mix it up for the participants by allowing them to talk to new people as often as feasible. This will honor the brilliance in the room.

Acknowledge the obvious. If something is a review, call it out and let people in the room who know the information become the experts.

Trust the learning is happening. You do not have to be the one to say the information for the participants to get it.

# NOTE-TAKING

Complete a 3, 2, 1 and add it to your notes.

What are *three* things that you learned in this chapter?

What are *two* things that you will utilize in your work?

What is *one* thing that you want to know more about moving forward?

# NEXT STEPS

Find ways to be your most authentic self. Do not hold back from your participants but instead lean in and let them see the real you. You are a pretty likable human; do not be afraid of that.

# Make Learning Logical

I have attended at least 150 training experiences in my career. Couple that with my undergraduate, master's, and doctoral degrees, and I have been in a ridiculous number of learning opportunities. Some were amazing. Some, well, sucked. They sucked for a variety of reasons, but a major one was how illogically the day was designed.

One time, I walked into a room for a full-day training in data analysis. Woohoo! Jealous, aren't you?

We sat down, not knowing what to expect, but we were already convinced it was going to be painful. For the next four hours, we worked with theoretical scenarios and made up numbers to learn different forms of data analysis. We did not work with our own teams, but instead broke up into random groups and worked through situations that did not relate to our own schools at all.

After the fourth hour, we took a break—the first break of the day. Our brains hurt, and we had no idea how to apply anything we had learned. The break ended; and we were handed our own school data and given exactly 30 minutes to analyze, using the new techniques, the only relevant data we had seen all day. Abruptly, the training ended, and we felt more clueless than when we had started.

What if, at the beginning of the day, we had been handed our own data instead of fake numbers?

What if the trainer had laid out clear objectives for what would be covered and let us come up with some goals for the day?

What if we took a break every hour or so to let the new information settle in our minds?

What if we worked with our school teams so that when we returned to campus we would have an idea of our actual next steps instead of hypothetical ones?

Learning needs to be logical, having clear, sound reasoning to back it up. When learning is logical the brain can file the information in a location that can be easily retrieved. If the learner struggles with the format of learning and the new content, chances are strong one or the other is not going to happen. The brain appreciates when topics make sense in the way they are presented.

Once the structure for the learning is established, a great facilitator will create opportunities for the learner to process what is being learned. This processing comes in multiple forms. Processing opportunities can be written or verbal, individual or collaborative, and can be enhanced through solid note taking and interacting. This is the time your daughter is learning Algebra or your employees learning Microsoft Suite.

When learning is logical the entire focus of the learning can be on the content.

Professional learning, even the kind that involves intense data analysis, does not have to be painful; it just must be logical.

# Structure

## MAKES LEARNING STICK

# NEED TO KNOW

- Create quality over quantity of information.
- Use energizers.
- Take breaks.
- Feed the participants.
- Reflect.

√ QUALITY

QUANTITY

No more Free Bird 11-minute guitar solos. Be intentional with your time and spend it wisely.

I need you to show our team how to do these 55 things tomorrow. You have two hours. Go.

Sound familiar? This happens all the time. Too much stuff and not enough time.

Prior to my current position I was a program specialist, and it was my job to train our internal staff so that what we delivered looked the same from California to Florida and everywhere in between. It was not unusual for me to be handed—no joke—20 topics, and the expectation included quality professional learning that covered every topic. There is no way that type of learning will stick.

Quality over quantity must be the mantra. That does not mean you can ignore 19 of the 20 items, but it does mean that prioritization and combination is key.

When designing a training, the structure of the day makes a huge difference. There is always too much content to cover in too little time, which leads to the participants feeling like they are drinking from a fire hose. The trainer, manager or lead learner is pressed for time and therefore spewing way more information than anyone can retain. Processing time and practice are the two most often cut items to cover all the material.

Well, guess what, none of the information will be retained if you cut out the processing time and practice. There is a successful way to structure the day so all the material can be covered, and participants will retain what they learned.

# NORMS

Setting norms at the beginning of a training sets the tone for the entire experience. Norms are guidelines the entire group agrees will make the training run more smoothly. These are not meant to be constrictive rules, but instead opportunities to bring structure and purpose back into the process.

Norms can either be set ahead of time or created collaboratively. Ask the room what needs to happen for this to be set in a great learning environment. There are some specific norms that work well in any environment, but you will need to pick and choose what makes sense for your audience.

I do not recommend more than five norms whenever possible. The norms should cover the following:

- Managing devices
- Implementing what is learned
- Asking questions
- Willingness to learn

It makes sense to put the norms at the beginning of the day, then get everyone to acknowledge them in some way to share their agreement.

Here are some examples:

**Be present.** This norm could include everything from managing devices (the struggle is real) to keeping sidebar conversations to a minimum. Participants sometimes need to be reminded not to be distracted by all that goes on outside the training room. It is completely acceptable to call out the fact you understand the participants have a life outside of the training session and may need to use their phones. I like to say to them, "You will get out of this training what you put into it, so I am asking you to be focused on the present as much as possible, while still taking care of your family." You can frame this norm to work for your situation.

**Be open-minded.** This norm helps participants to remember that everything said may not sit well with their current way of work, but it is important to try to accept the new opportunity. It is important participants use what they learned back in their work environment, so this one carries extra weight.

**Be positive.** In every single situation there is a good and a bad. You have a choice to focus on either one. Your focus will determine what you see most. Encourage your participants to focus on the good.

Be respectful, be responsible, be a problem solver, take risks, use new learning, the list goes on. Think about what you need participants to do, then select the norms that are appropriate for your audience.

You want to keep a positive spin on norms for adults. Avoid phrases that start with "don't", i.e. Don't talk when someone else is talking. Don't use your phone during the training. When we tell someone not to do something, instinctively he/she will want to do the opposite.

Setting norms is just as valuable in the office daily. If acceptable and unacceptable behavior is not clearly outlined, it is difficult to hold people accountable for their behavior at all. Although most organizations have unspoken norms, clear is kind. Be clear with the norms and expectations and post them somewhere easily visible.

One-on-one norms are valuable too. Talk through expectations together prior to your interactions. If you are a floor nurse teaching a newer nurse his new role, set some expectations up front for how those interactions will go. Be sure when working one on one that both of you agree to the norms being created. Both parties need to offer up some suggestions to ensure that the interactions run smoothly.

List your preferred norms below. What new ones do you wish to add?

WRITE YOUR THOUGHTS HERE:

# ENERGIZERS: BRAIN & BODY

Have you ever been in a training and literally nodded off? You probably squirmed in your seat, searched your bag for a piece of candy or gum, and maybe even went to the bathroom, just to stay awake. As a facilitator, you can see this happening in the room. When you look around, are people engaged or exhausted?

Never underestimate the power of a break. People are busy. They have personal and professional lives going on outside of this training. You must give space for people to check in with the outside world. In addition to checking in,

Get music ideas:
LearningCanStick.com

they need to check out of the learning every so often as well. A good rule of thumb is for every 60-90 minutes of instruction there is a 10-15 minute break.

Play music during the break to help spark conversation and camaraderie. Something upbeat works well if you want them to be excited when they return. When you want to calm them after a particularly taxing segment, use classical music. Cater to the audience's needs.

In addition to a body break, sometimes you just need a brain break. These take only about 2 minutes, but they give you a chance to clear your head and start to digest the information being shared. The increase of oxygen to your brain allows you to absorb new information. Brain breaks can be silly or topical. Both work well, you just need to consider your audience.

Here are some examples of total physical response breaks.

- Spell something with different body parts. Have them write their first name in the air with their right pointer finger. Then have them write their middle name with their left foot. Then, my personal favorite, have them write their last name with their rear end. This one is hilarious; and remember, emotions equal learning.

- Office yoga can be easy and fun. If your company name is an acronym or fairly short, have the participants make the shape of the letters with their bodies. For example, an I is both hands straight over head, or an A is hands together overhead and feet spread apart.

- Standing on consonants and sitting on vowels can be effective and quick. Pick a word on the screen everyone can see. Spell the word out loud and stand when there is a consonant and sit when there is a vowel. CoLLaBoRaTioN for example.

- Allow people to stand and share one piece of information they have learned in the last session with a partner. Sharing can also be a brain break if it involves a state change, such as sitting to standing.

Be sensitive to those who cannot physically stand or perform what you are asking of them. If they cannot stand, have them raise their arms above their heads. Be aware of your audience's needs and their capabilities.

# MOVEMENT

Movement is mandatory for memories to form. At least once an hour, the participants need to move. The movement can be just a simple stand to share your idea, but it must happen. It does not take any longer to debrief in a standing position than it does in a seated position; but by standing, blood flow increases to the brain, in turn activating memory cells. Use the brain breaks above as suggestions. Be sure to write them into your notes, or you will forget to include them. It takes 18 times of trying these things for them to become a habit. Simple cues will help.

Consider when in the day you are presenting the most brain taxing information. There are a couple sweet spots in every training. The second hour of an all-day training is a perfect place to put a heavy thinking opportunity. The minds in the room are still fresh but the initial settling in has already taken place.

Beware of the post lunch lull. Whatever you plan to teach after lunch, make sure it is interactive. Do not have the group reading and analyzing numbers after a big meal. There is a very natural lull in energy after lunch because all the ATP in our bodies are in the stomach working on digesting our food instead of being in our brains. Instead, put activities here that require people to move around.

Want a couple ways to get people moving while still covering new information?

## WALK AND TALK

Put participants into partners and give them a topic to discuss. This could be a preview into a new topic or a review of the previous topic. Give them a set amount of time and a loose parameter of the property then let them go. The goal is they are walking for the duration of the conversation. They can go outside or stay inside; they just have to keep moving. This works great for all ages of learners. Try it with your own children.

## STAND AND SHARE

Instead of just sharing information with a partner at the table, have everyone in the room stand up and find a partner from another table. They will stand while they share their thoughts with their partner. When both partners have finished sharing, both will sit. Now you have increased the oxygen to their brains, and when everyone is seated you will have an instant cue to move on to the next topic.

## FIND A NEW SPOT

Ask participants to find a new spot in the room for the next learning opportunity. It can be on the floor, on a table, in a chair or in the hallway, but it must be different from where they have been for the majority of the training. This new spot will do two things. It will give a new perspective to the learner, and it will create a new "file" in the participants brain.

Where we are when we learn something determines where information is filed in our brains. If we are always in the same spot when learning, our file folder never changes; and that file gets quite full. When it is time to retrieve information, your brain must sort through the entire file folder of information. Instead, by switching it up, you have reduced the amount of time your brain has to search for the new information.

People are territorial and tend to want to stay in one place for an entire training. Wherever they sit on day one will be where they sit for the remaining days unless you intentionally move them around. You will have to create opportunities to move them from their home base. It is okay for the movement to be temporary, but it does need to happen throughout the day to create those new file folders of information.

Bonus, it keeps the boredom at bay.

What is one way you will get participants moving during your next training?

WRITE YOUR THOUGHTS HERE:

## SPACE OUT THE CONTENT

Trainers often talk to an audience for 30-45 minutes without pausing for understanding or processing. The brain stops listening after roughly 10 minutes. You can get back on track and listen again, but you are going to miss something as your brain chases a proverbial "squirrel."

Remember in the movie *Up*, when Dug the dog would be mid-sentence and then notice a squirrel. That concept is more relevant than you could

imagine when teaching adult learners. We have so many different ideas, responsibilities, and needs floating through our minds at any given moment that, when we get overwhelmed with new information, we will naturally chase a "squirrel" just for a break.

For every 10 minutes of direct instruction there should be at least two minutes of processing time. This tactic is frequently underestimated or overlooked altogether. In the group of leaders I surveyed, I learned the lack of processing time is an equal frustration for education and business leaders. If you do not give space and time for processing, both individually and collaboratively, the information gets lost and therefore forgotten.

Processing time can be given in a variety of ways.

- Two minutes to write down notes about what they just heard.
- Two minutes to discuss what they learned with a partner.
- Two minutes to talk as a table group about what was just discussed. (This might take 4 minutes since there are more people.)

Please do not skip this. The number one frustration when learning new information is the lack of processing time. Trainers often say there is just too much to cover to give processing time.

Reality check, you can cover all the information you wish; but without processing time, the participants will not learn it. With processing time, their retention of the new material will go up dramatically, increasing the likelihood of implementation after the training.

## SNACKS

Our brains burn more calories than any other part of our bodies. This is why we can sit at a desk and not get up, working and thinking, and be completely exhausted at the end of the day. Your brain needs two things to continue to function—oxygen and food. There are lots of different types of fuel you can provide, but some are more popular than others.

Candy does not give long-term energy, but it can give the right-now pick me up needed to power through to a break. Chocolate is the crowd favorite, typically, but hard candies work well too. Be considerate of allergies and try to have a variety of options.

Granola bars are another excellent option because they are individually wrapped and typically have some protein for sustainability. They are not always as popular as candy but are certainly better for the participants and their long-term energy situation. Again, avoid allergenic options.

If training is taking place in a convention center or hotel you often cannot bring in outside foods. If this is the case, be strategic about when the catered food arrives and what is served. Avoid super heavy carbohydrate foods for lunch. This makes the participants sleepy. Also space out snacks so there is an option for nourishment every couple hours. Everyone will not choose to partake, but having the option will help keep their attention.

## TIMING

Always give an extra 15 minutes of padding to your agenda. Less is more. These extra fifteen minutes will mean the difference between feeling overwhelmed at the end of a training and feeling saturated at the end of a training. Don't just build it into the end of the day. Instead add a couple minutes more to each activity than you believe you will need. If your anticipated timing was accurate, you will have the gift of time at the end of the day for additional reflection. If you underestimated how long it would take to get things done, you will end right on time.

## SAMPLE ONE-HOUR AGENDA

| Time | Activities/ Topics | Supplies | Explanation |
|---|---|---|---|
| 5 minutes | Welcome and Purpose Norms | Slide or agenda item | Regardless of time constraints, always start with "good things" at the beginning of a meeting to set the tone. Remind the team of the norms you have set. |
| 15 minutes | Topic 1 | A visual to anchor understanding (one-page document with all the most pertinent information for the meeting and space to take notes) | Start with the more difficult topic so that people's minds are fresh and ready to absorb the new information. |
| 2-3 minutes | Process Topic 1 | Time to talk to others or process alone | Keep reading for processing ideas. |
| 2-3 minutes | Questions about Topic 1 | A way to capture the ideas: white board, Google slide, chart paper, Teams chat | Let the learners talk. This will save time in the long run. |
| 15 minutes | Topic 2 | A visual to anchor understanding | This might be an easier topic or a connection to the last topic. |
| 2-3 minutes | Process Topic 2 | Time to talk to others or process alone | Always process the learning! |
| 2-3 minutes | Questions about Topic 2 | A way to capture the ideas: white board, Google slide, chart paper, Teams chat | Questions allow for deeper understanding. |
| 15 minutes | New Topic or Activity using the first 2 Topics | Include space for making connections on the learning tool. | Avoid too many new ideas at once. Make connections whenever possible so that the learner sees how things fit together. |
| 5 minutes | Next Steps | List of action items | Always end a meeting with clear action items/next steps from the team. |

## SAMPLE ALL-DAY AGENDA

| Time | Activities/ Topics | Supplies | Explanation |
|---|---|---|---|
| 15 minutes | Welcome and Purpose | Slide | I always include at least 15minutes to start the day. People are going to be late and/or will need extra time to settle in. Plan for it. |
| 10 minutes | Objectives Overview of the Day Norms | Slide with objectives clearly posted | These topics set the tone for the day and let participants know what to expect in the training. Clear is kind. |
| 45-60 minutes | Topic 1 - Include at least one energizer. | Handouts and slides | Topic one can be a heavy hitter, but still needs to be interactive. |
| 10 minutes | BREAK | Music Coffee | Do not skip breaks. |
| 60-90 minutes | Topic 1 continued or Topic 2 - Include at least one energizer. - Let the participants do the talking. - Have a reflection opportunity for the learning thus far. | Handouts and slides | This time frame can be a continuation of the last topic or a new topic. Participants are still focused at this point during the day, and this activity/topic can take you through to lunch if need be. |
| 60 minutes | LUNCH | Food | If lunch can be catered that is ideal. If people leave to get lunch, it is difficult to get them back on time. |
| 60-90 minutes | Topic 3 - Include at least 2 energizers. - Avoid long reading activities or sitting still for too long right after lunch. | Handouts and slides | This is the toughest time slot of the day. Keep the participants active with intentionality. Consider specific opportunities to incorporate movement and/ or high-energy strategies here. |

## SAMPLE ALL-DAY AGENDA

| Time | Activities/ Topics | Supplies | Explanation |
|---|---|---|---|
| 10 minutes | BREAK | Music Snacks | Consider not serving dessert with lunch but saving it for this time slot. |
| 45-60 minutes | Topic 3 continued or Topic 4 Include at least 1 energizer. Begin reviewing previous learning. | Handouts and slides | Less is often more. Three major ideas are plenty for a training. Four is doable if they are all related. |
| 10 minutes | BREAK | Music Snacks | Snack could go here instead. Not necessary to happen at both breaks. Maybe just some caffeine options. |
| 45-60 minutes | Review and Reflect Next Steps | Handouts and slides | Recap the entire day. Revisit main ideas. Ask participants to reflect on learning. Always include action steps to do upon returning to work. |

These examples are structured for a one or six-hour training; but the concept can be abbreviated, lengthened, or repeated to meet your needs.

# NEED TO KNOW

Create quality over quantity of information. Be intentional with what you choose to share.

Use energizers because it increases oxygen to the brain and makes learning stick.

Take breaks to increase attention and retention. Having a little space in the day to digest information allows for creativity and learning to happen.

Feed the participants. We cannot think if we are hungry.

Take time to reflect. This is how we make learning personal.

# NOTE-TAKING

Build a sample agenda with some topics you know are coming up soon. How will you use this chapter to shape your future trainings? What specific tip resonated with you; how will you use it, and how will that tip influence your next interaction with learners?

# NEXT STEPS

Build the kind of training you yourself would want to attend. If it feels painful to you, it will absolutely be painful to your participants. Build a structurally sound day full of breaks, thoughtfulness, and "strategery."

# Synthesis

## MAKES LEARNING STICK

# NEED TO KNOW

- Create note interactions.
- Utilize one-page summaries.
- Allow for verbal recaps of learning.

# NOTE-TAKING WITH INTERACTIONS

Information cannot stick unless the person learning the information interacts with that information. Interactions can happen in a variety of ways, and a great facilitator can orchestrate those interactions. A great facilitator recognizes the need for processing and provides it throughout the training opportunity. These interactions will not happen without some intentional orchestration, however.

I was a biology major when I got my undergraduate degree, and I attended Catawba College in Salisbury, North Carolina. It is a beautiful, small liberal arts school in the heart of North Carolina. I knew the moment I stepped on campus I was meant to spend four years there. It suited me.

From the time I was in kindergarten, I wanted to become a teacher. Again, it just suited me. As the years went on, I decided I really wanted to teach high school. My favorite subjects in school were English and biology, so I figured I would teach one of those. When my senior English teacher, Mrs. Charlsie Brown, found out I wanted to be a teacher she asked me if I wanted to spend the rest of my life grading papers. I said, "Not really;" and she said, "Then teach anything but English." Ironically, I am now an adjunct professor who most often teaches the major case study, which means I spend a lot of my time grading papers. I guess a part of me really likes grading papers.

Mrs. Brown did convince me, however, to teach biology instead of English. I decided I could make biology exciting and fun! In order to become a high school teacher though, I had to major in my subject matter and minor in secondary education. Everyone else in my major wanted to be a doctor. They loved cells, microorganisms, formulas and labs. I just loved teaching and the science was required to make that happen.

In order to graduate with a biology degree, it was required I take organic chemistry. I am 100% convinced Satan himself wrote organic chemistry. I hated everything about that course. In fact, it wasn't until the second semester of organic chemistry 2 was almost over that I discovered the little color-coded things I had drawn every day in his class were actually reactions, and the different colors represented where the different molecules went when they were combined. To put it into context for my non-science friends, the entire premise of organic chemistry is chemical reactions with carbon. Everything he talked about was based on that. Basically, I missed the exact point of the class and I was clueless.

It was not for lack of trying that I was clueless, however. I sat in the very front seat of the middle row and attended every single class. I always arrived early, and I would have four different colored pens so my notes would match the professor's notes.

I should mention, our professor had written the organic chemistry textbook! His gift was understanding reactions, not teaching. I would write down absolutely everything that man said or wrote. Then, I would go back to my room and slide my notebook under my bed until the next class. The day before a test I would look at those notes a little more closely, cry because I did not understand anything I was reading, and then promptly fail the tests.

I did not get it. I was writing everything down. I was trying desperately to pay attention. I wanted to learn. I honestly just didn't know how to learn. I thought writing down the professor's thoughts and ideas was enough. The problem was I never made those notes my own.

Note-taking is only step one of the learning process. The most often neglected yet much more integral step is making those notes your own.

What if I had gone back to my dorm room and taken the time to rewrite the notes a second time? Or I could have written notes on the notes. Or I could have compared them to my roommate's notes. Or I could have written questions in the margin I thought the professor might ask on the next test. Making notes your own means interacting with them in a way that burns the information into your brain.

Trainings are not often followed by tests, although some could be. (think compliance, recertification, etc.) More often, they are followed by an expectation that the learning be used in a work setting. How much better might that learning stick if there was an expectation of the participants making the notes they take in a training their own?

As a facilitator, there are so many ways this processing and interaction could happen. Dr. Beard, my organic chemistry professor, was a brilliant man who completely understood everything about his subject matter. He did all the talking in class, which meant at the end of class, he knew even more about organic chemistry than when he started. Meanwhile, most of us were left behind, not interacting with the content at all.

A great facilitator of learning recognizes that the learners need to process the information they are hearing. This processing must happen more than once, and it likely needs to happen in more than one way. Written processing is great, but so is verbal processing. Here are a couple ideas for how written processing could take place so your participants are more successful at learning your content than I was learning organic chemistry.

What if you allotted five minutes at the end of each segment of the day for participants to take time to revisit and revise their notes? Sometimes it is just a lack of time preventing people from doing this crucial step when learning. During these five minutes, you could put a prompt on the projector guiding their thinking back to your objectives. A gentle reminder of what they were supposed to have learned during that chunk of time will help focus the interaction with their notes.

Do not overthink how to structure this time, but do not underestimate its value either. During the last minute of the five, let them share their notes with someone else and highlight their biggest takeaways from the learning. This will boost accountability for them to stay on task during the five minutes, and it will increase the success of the processing because they had to share their ideas with someone else. This is what was missing from my note-taking experience in organic chemistry—the chance to discuss my learning as well as my understanding of the learning with my peers. I should have done it on my own, but I did not know this was something I needed. Create space for this with your participants. The difference will be immediate and long lasting.

## THE ONE-PAGE SUMMARY

Sometimes it is more than just time, though, that prevents people from processing their learning. Sometimes, it is a lack of knowing how to synthesize the learning.

Here is an excellent way to get people to synthesize their learning.

The one-page summary.

This is my favorite tool for turning a large quantity of information into bite-sized chunks.

At the end of the day of training, or at the end of a section that needs to be remembered, ask the participants to capture the key information onto a one-page document for their own learning purposes. This one-page document could hang in their offices for reference and guide them back to their learning quickly and easily. It can be an individual creation, or it can be done in small groups to further deepen the learning.

The end result of this process is a one-page reference sheet that will remind learners of the topics of the training and what to do with what they learned now that they are back at work.

There are a couple important components in this process. You can mix and match these to best suit the topic at hand. You do not need to include every component every time, but do encourage variety of thought.

Encourage creativity and uniqueness in this process. Maybe even make it a competition. The best one gets replicated for the rest of the office. Often bragging rights are enough to make the competition worthwhile. These components are not mandatory, but they are helpful if you want the learning to stick.

1. Include key vocabulary, with definitions.

2. Require a graphic representation (aka picture). This might be a graphic depiction of a cycle of events or a process or procedure. Even if they cannot draw, using art accesses a different portion of the brain which changes where and how the information is stored.

3. Ask for synthesis of the information. Maybe this is a three-sentence summary or a reflection on the learning, but it is for sure short and sweet.

4. Include a specific opportunity for the learner to determine how the information will be utilized. This could be a couple sentences or a picture explaining the use of the knowledge.

5.      Tap into creativity. Use color, art, and fun. This should not just be words on a page, but a synthesis of learning. It can be done electronically or by hand, depending on your audience.

6.      Give a short time constraint. You are trying to push them to capture the important parts of their learning. Too much time just allows the participants to overthink. A great one-pager can be created in 10 minutes. If you check in after 10 minutes and they are not yet done, give them a couple more; but let them feel the pressure of the clock. That is often when we do our best work.

After the one-pagers are created, give people a chance to see one another's products. It is incredibly beneficial to see what other people thought was valuable enough to mention. You will quickly see which points were most fully understood and which ones might need to be revisited. This will help you, as the facilitator, determine what you have left to cover or where you could be a little more specific next time.

Make sure everyone in each group leaves with a copy of their one-page summary. Just have them take pictures. It is beneficial if they want to take pictures of all of them. You could also use something like Photo Circle to have a common place to share these new ideas and artifacts like these. Photo Circle is a free app that allows a group of people to share pictures. There are many other ways to do this, but what makes Photo Circle easy is you can share a code with a large group of people and all they have to do is enter it. Everyone automatically has permission to upload and see the other pictures.

As I have mentioned throughout this book, the person doing the talking is the person doing the learning. Another way to get your participants to synthesize information is to create space for them to talk about it. At the end of each segment of learning, make sure the participants have a chance to talk to someone else about their understanding of the content.

They should have the chance to switch up who they talk with as much as possible. The conversation does not have to be incredibly structured; it just needs to happen. Give a sentence prompt and let them do the rest. Here are some suggestions.

Please share two things you learned with someone at your table.

Please repeat something you heard me say to someone near you.

Share something you learned in the last 30 minutes you will use at work in the next two weeks.

Trust they will stay on topic. Limit the amount of time they talk to about three to four minutes, depending on the topic. Just like with the one-page summary, feeling the pressure of time will focus the conversation. At the end of the four minutes ask if there are any questions. Typically, the questions are now more focused and specific than they would have been before people had a chance to process with one another.

Note-taking, note-processing, one-page creations and repeating information out loud all work in one-on-one situations as well. If you have a therapy patient who is going to be on a new regime, don't take the notes for him; let him do it, if he is able. Ask him to repeat the process to you. Have him create a one-page summary of the physical therapy prescription, complete with pictures. The chances of his knowing exactly how to do the exercises will go up dramatically, because he made the information his own.

# NEED TO KNOW

Create note interactions to improve retention of information. Find ways for participants to interact with their notes after they are taken.

Utilize one-page summaries to create opportunities for participants to synthesize information, either alone or with others. Create time for it to happen.

Allow for verbal recaps of learning to create strong processing and understanding of information. Build these into your trainings.

# NOTE-TAKING

Create a one-pager including your takeaways from this chapter, complete with a graphic representation of your learning.

# NEXT STEPS

How will you build in opportunities to synthesize and process new learning during your training?

What opportunities will you build in to improve the learning of those who are in your sessions?

# CHAPTER

# 4

# Make Learning Fun

I bet you have not had a participant turn a cartwheel in a ballroom during a training session. I have. A principal, no less.

It was 4:00 pm and we started at 8:00 am. We were all tired, and we had an hour to go. I was training using a syllabus designed by someone else; and apparently, she thought having a group of 80 people number off one to five then read different portions of a document based on that number was a good plan that late in the day. She was wrong.

I decided to spice things up a bit. I told the room leaders that they needed to number off one to five, but they needed to make it memorable. Actually, I said they needed to make it epic, so that others would be able to remember their number.

The very first person stood up in her chair did a wave from one hand to the other and sang "one." That is exactly what I am talking about. Epic. We worked our way around the room, some numbers in Spanish, some in opera tones, each person trying to outdo the last. I could see the people on the other side of the room studying those before them, trying to be the best.

In the back of the room, one gentleman gave me a big number one, with an inappropriate finger, and the room was in stitches. Then we got to a woman who was not going to be outdone. She jumped up, ran to the side of the hotel ballroom and turned not one, not two, but three cartwheels. I literally dropped the mic. The energy in the room was electric. The fun meter was off the charts. And it was 4:15 pm after a long day of learning.

We not only had a renewed sense of excitement, but not a single participant tried to sneak out early. The leaders had amazing conversations about that article, and they continued the conversation long after the session was over.

When emotion is involved in learning the likelihood we will remember the information increases. Creating an environment that stirs up emotion helps learners enjoy their learning experience.

Happiness and resilience are directly correlated. In order to be a successful learner, one must exhibit resilience and a willingness to be flexible. If you can evoke happiness in the learner, resilience will follow.

It might not be an actual cartwheel, but how can you get your participants to turn some emotional cartwheels in your presence?

It is time to get everyone to sing along, my karaoke master. I hear lots of ba, ba, ba's in your near future.

# Emotion

## MAKES LEARNING STICK

## NEED TO KNOW

- Use humor to break the ice.
- Be okay with a little silly.
- Use music.

# EMOTIONS=LEARNING

Our emotions drive our actions, but they also attach to our memories. If you can evoke emotion in participants, their memories become activated.

Do you remember what you did on September 11, 2001? I absolutely do. I was walking out of my house in Salisbury, NC, heading to the hospital to see my sister-in-law in ICU. We had five-month-old twins. It was a beautiful day, and our family was all together. Our neighbor walked out of his house and asked me if I had seen the news. I had not, and he proceeded to tell me a plane had flown into the first tower. I remember looking at him and saying, "Weren't there people in there?" The shock and barrage of emotions meant I remembered everything about that day. I remember what my babies were wearing, how we worried about my father-in-law who was back in Florida and had flown home the day before, how I had to tutor that night and did not know what to say to my student. That day was full of emotions, which meant my brain retained it all. I bet you could tell me every detail of your experience that day too.

Now, do you remember what you did on June 12, 1999? Probably not, right. You might know you brushed your teeth, at least we hope you did; but that is about it. Yet, again, I remember everything about that day. That is the day I married my best friend. Emotions equal learning and memory.

### *How does this apply to professional development?*

If you can find ways to evoke emotion in your participants, they are much more likely to remember what you taught them. Our brains associate learning with emotion. We categorize information differently depending on how we felt when we learned it.

When we feel safe, we are free to process and remember information. When we are amused, we connect the learning to positive feelings. When we laugh, we remember. When we cry, we learn. I do not recommend making your participants cry, but I do recommend making them feel.

## USE HUMOR

Humor can break down walls and create almost instant bonds. Humor cannot come at someone else's expense; but it can lighten the mood and connect learning to emotion, making it stick. The best way to do this as a facilitator is to laugh at yourself. Do not be afraid to be vulnerable. Laugh when you make a mistake. Joke about the fact most of the room was "voluntold" to be at the training. Make light of the fact they are taking CPR for the tenth time in their career. Your willingness to make them feel will also make them learn.

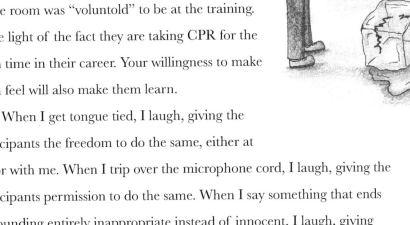

When I get tongue tied, I laugh, giving the participants the freedom to do the same, either at me or with me. When I trip over the microphone cord, I laugh, giving the participants permission to do the same. When I say something that ends up sounding entirely inappropriate instead of innocent, I laugh, giving participants the chance to do the same.

The more light-hearted you can be in a learning scenario, the more likely your participants will remember what happened. I am not suggesting you make light of the material, just that you are light-hearted in the delivery of the material. You want your audience to take you seriously, but you have already established credibility. Now you need them to want to be invested in the learning, which calls for a little more fun.

## CELEBRATE SILLY WINS

I realize I just said you want your audience to take you seriously, but that does not mean you cannot have fun.

I have been training adults for about 14 years, and I have learned some things hold true regardless of the make-up of the participants. Whether working with educators, medical professionals, business leaders or entrepreneurs, adults carry the weight of the world on their shoulders. If you can lighten the load, even temporarily, learning can happen. I am often amazed at how something corny wins people over. Here is something worth trying. Hang with me on this one, it is tried and true.

Consider ways to celebrate your participants. When someone shares a great idea, or participates in an activity, or just needs some kudos, they should be celebrated. Our typical celebration would be to clap for them. This often feels disingenuous because participants will be half-hearted with their applause after one or two participants. What if, instead of regular applause after a great suggestion or idea, you said let's give a 1, 2, 3, clap. Then you count 1, 2, 3, and everyone claps once, all together.

This feels more celebratory and creates camaraderie. You certainly can keep it simple or consistent throughout the training. Maybe you give snaps instead of claps. Stay authentic to your personality but celebrate your participants.

You could really get crazy with fun claps if you want.

Here are just a few to pique your interest.

Full Clap Video:
LearningCanStick.com

| CLAPS | DESCRIPTIONS |
|---|---|
| 123 Clap | Facilitator counts one, two, three then everyone claps once. |
| Snaps | Simply snap instead of clap. |
| Silent Cheer | In sign language, applause is both hands up in the air turned back and forth. |
| Boom Boom Clap | Think, We Will Rock You. Count to 3 then bang the table twice and clap once. |
| Clap Clap Clap | Count to 3 then clap three times. |
| Firework | Rub your hands together and shimmy them up like a firework, then clap at the top and snap your fingers on the way down. Be sure to "ohh and ahh" at the fireworks. |
| Sparkler | Choose one finger (be sure it is an appropriate finger) and use the other hand to snap all around that finger like a sparkler on the 4th of July. |
| Bubble Gum | Place your hands in front of your mouth and "blow the bubble" three times then clap your hands together…because clearly the bubble burst. |
| Rubber Band | Pull your hands away from one another as if you had a rubber band around them. Then let go and clap rapidly like the rubber band snapped back together. |
| Snap Crackle Pop | Go back to a bowl of Rice Krispies. First snap, then "crackle" by rubbing your hands together, then pop by clapping once. Be sure to say "snap, crackle, pop" while you do it. |
| Fantastic | Think Fantastic cleaning solution. Spray it three times then wipe it off in a circle while saying "fantastic." You can do a Spanish version if you wish, just say Fabuloso. |

Know your audience with the claps. Not every room will warm up to the silly instantly, but you would be shocked at how different groups respond. Emotion works. Be okay with a little silliness.

I once had a participant who absolutely did not want to be in my training. This gentleman was a bodybuilder, with arms as big as my legs; and he sat with those giant arms folded across his chest and a scowl on his face for the first three days of our five days together. I am over the top when I present, complete with enthusiasm, stickers, laughter, and all the claps listed above. On day three, this gentleman raised his hand and said, "Christie, I've got one for you." I looked at him in shock and said, "One what…a clap?" He said, "Yep." I literally leapt in the air with excitement and said, "Please share!"

He stood up, swiped his hands together as if distributing papers in an arch over his head, and threw his hands up, letting them cascade down. The room loved it. I learned later, this gesture is called "making it rain." I had no idea what that meant; I was just so excited he was willing to participate. I immediately made the whole room repeat the motion. People were cracking up, and I had no idea why. I am not a complete moron, but I am somewhat naïve sometimes.

For those of you who read "make it rain" and knew what it meant, you completely understand why this was so hilarious to the majority of the room. If you do not know what it means, go ahead and Google it. To me, I just went all in because I was making a connection with a participant. My training partner pulled me aside during the break and told me what it meant, and I was mortified!! I promise I would never have made the entire room do something like that. Ever.

And yet, that gentleman fully participated for the rest of our time together. He laughed, he learned, he loved it all. I got him to laugh, even though it was totally at my expense, and that allowed him to learn. I tell that story because we all need a little more laughter. Interestingly enough, that moment shifted the momentum of the entire group. Even though that training happened eight years ago, people still reach out to me from that group to ask questions; and I know that the learning stuck. Emotion increases our ability to grow.

## AVOID SARCASM BUT BE WITTY

Using sarcasm is incredibly tempting with adult learners. The problem with sarcasm is someone is always the victim. In the story above, I suppose I was a bit of a victim; but I was also the trainer, and he was the participant. He had learned who I authentically was over three days' time, and knew he was safe with me. He also recognized this was needed for him to fully participate.

You do not know your audience well enough even after a few hours or days to know what is and is not acceptable to them in terms of banter. Instead of sarcasm, be quick witted. Even corny jokes work. Or play music tied to the activity you are doing. For example, when you ask people to interact with one another, play, "I'm So Excited." Or when you are going to write a reflection on what they have learned, play, "Man in the Mirror." Your participants will appreciate the wit and creative thinking.

Humor that fits with the industry is often most popular. Save up the corny jokes about procedures, medicine, sales teams, and HR and find strategic places to drop them into your day. You might have to write them into your script at first but soon they will come a little more naturally.

In any training, you will have people who are sure they already know it all, and maybe they do know a lot about the topic. Humor can often break down the façade and allow people to be real. My muscular friend who did not want to engage needed to break down the façade, and he did so with humor. I know it was good hearted. He told me after he made it rain he had been listening and absorbing the information all along. The scowl was his thinking face. But he later admitted he learned a lot more in the last two days, when he allowed himself to be fully invested in the learning.

What "shop" humor will your audience appreciate, and how can you throw that in? My mom works in the funeral business, pre-selling all arrangements. She will often say people are "dying to come see her." That sounds horrible to most of us, but people in that business laugh every time.

## THEMES

Emotion can be evoked in a variety of ways. Another tried and true way to get people emotionally invested is to involve themes into your time together. Themes can be as simple or complex as you wish to make them.

Think about the topics included in your training. Are you trying to create space for unity? Are you teaching people how to coach their employees? Are you trying to spark creativity? I do not know what your themes will be, but I do know how to make them memorable.

During that same training where the gentleman taught me how to "make it rain," my training partner and I had themes for each day.

One of the days was spent teaching the participants how to become coaches. We started by dressing the part. This will not always be appropriate, but it can take things to a whole new level. We wore sweat bands and matching polos, and we had whistles. We gave each participant a whistle when he or she came into the room. There was no way anyone in our room that day walked away without knowing the topic of conversation. It was literally in their face, around their necks and embedded throughout the day. We all became coaches that day. Even our music stayed on theme. We played songs like "Eye of the Tiger" and "We are the Champions" for transitions and breaks.

I know everyone did not catch every nuance, but we kept coaching in their subconscious all day long. They left feeling equipped to coach, and they had a whistle to remind them they are coaches, who shepherd success in employees through actions and words.

You should not explain your themes to the participants. Instead, ask them to try to figure it out themselves. I promise what they come up with is often better than your original idea. If they do not get around to the point you were making, certainly tell them what you were thinking; or just go with their great ideas. This act of wrestling with the concept will increase their emotional investment to the content and will increase the stickiness.

Some other themes that might translate into your world are listed below. Think about how you might use these in your next training. The list includes things you might give participants at the door as they come into the training, music, and ideas for the day.

| TOPIC | THEME |
|---|---|
| Unity<br>Collaboration<br>Teamwork | Puzzle pieces<br>We are better together, and without everyone on board the puzzle simply isn't complete.<br>Songs:<br>"We Go Together" (Grease)<br>"Friends"<br>"Lean on Me"<br>"You've Got a Friend in Me" |
| Change | Hypercolor sticker/shirt/trinket<br>Different colors of the same token<br>Yin/Yang symbols<br>Change happens when we are not expecting it, and sometimes it is uncomfortable; but there is predictability and control as well. |

| TOPIC | THEME |
|---|---|
| Victory<br>Winning<br>Teamwork<br>Success | Medal<br>Trophy<br>Your success is our success. We want you to win. We believe in your abilities.<br>"We are the Champions"<br>"Celebrate Good Times"<br>"I Gotta Feeling"<br>"Don't Stop Believing" |
| Coaching | Whistles<br>Sweatbands (with your logo on them)<br>Short coaching shorts (okay, maybe not, depends on your audience)<br>A coach is a guide who works to make you better at everything you do.<br>"Chariots of Fire"<br>"You Raise Me Up" |

When doing this, I like to pick a trinket that will fit in their name badge or can be worn. If the trinket is something that will go on the table, it will likely be left there and forgotten. If you are at a larger conference, this type of bling on the name badge makes others jealous, which is an extra bonus when you are trying to make people feel a sense of belonging and worth.

Recently, I popped into a training session for our organization and had lunch with some of the participants. One lady kept staring at me as if trying to place why she knew me. After lunch, she pulled me aside and said,

*"I figured out why I know you. Five years ago, when I started on this journey, you were my trainer. You gave us a puzzle piece and reminded us our part in the puzzle of implementation was crucial. I still have my puzzle piece and I have used this same activity with my staff members multiple times. I love knowing I am a part of something bigger. Thank you for being such an influential trainer."*

Wow! I was so humbled she remembered me. It was not just what I said, but how I said it and what I did with it that made it stick for her. Her statement is a great testament to the fact that these ideas work. If you make people feel something when you work with them, they will remember. I, personally, choose to make sure that something is positive. We remember the bad too; but we, as the facilitators, have control over how much of the bad we create. I recommend avoiding it all together.

I have done this sort of emotion evoking fun with a variety of audiences and it really does always work. You will have a few who think it is elementary but most buy in right away. Creating a sense of belonging immediately makes participants feel they are part of something bigger.

I once conducted a training for about 80 administrators. These people were mostly principals and assistant principals, and everyone in the room was a leader. We had themes for each day and made sure we gave them something when they walked in the room to make them feel they belonged. We gave them a puzzle piece, superhero stickers, and a medal. We also gave stickers throughout the training when they shared great ideas or had ah-ha moments.

On the final day of the training, we spent some time reflecting on what people had learned that they would use with their staff members. One principal raised his hand and asked to address the room. He said,

*"From the minute we walked into this room, you have been blinging us out. At first, I was uncomfortable; but as the time wore on, I found myself getting excited to see what the next experience would be. It reminded me to have fun with my staff members and make them feel valued. I plan to start having themes for my meetings to stir up excitement and joy. Short of showering us in glitter, you pulled out all the stops and taught me to have fun again. I can't wait to try it this year!"*

We did actually shower him with glitter later that day. It is not about the glitter, although oddly effective. It is about the celebration. The love. The sense of belonging. We made sure people knew why they were there and then felt as if they did not want to leave. Most people are "voluntold" they have to attend training, but it is your job to make them be glad they came.

I surveyed all my leader friends, in both business and education, and asked them what their biggest struggles were when training adults. Several themes emerged with this question as well. The most frequent response, however, was creating buy in. You have to make people not only want to attend the training but learn something while they are there. These little nuances are really not so little. They are huge when setting the tone for others to feel comfortable.

## MUSIC

We talked a little about music in the Authenticity section, but there are so many ways it can be used. Music can be a total game changer! If you have upbeat, familiar, cross-age-groups-and-genres playlists going when people come into the room, the entire tone of the training changes before you even open your mouth. People are tapping their feet or singing along, bonding immediately. The music also serves as a safe background for conversation. It is much more difficult to have a conversation with a stranger in a silent room. You feel like everyone can hear you, therefore it is easier to stay quiet. The music creates a safe backdrop for conversation.

There are perfect beats for various situations. Faster tempos for conversation, slower for thinking. Instrumental only when trying to get people to think. In fact, I wrote this entire book while listening to instrumental praise music. I just go with my gut rather than stressing about whether or not a song fits the beat perfectly.

I want the music to evoke emotion. Every song I pick fits with the theme of that topic, as mentioned earlier. This creates variety and gets people to focus a little more on what is playing to see if they can figure out the theme.

I use the music to fill the gaps. I have it playing before we start. I have it playing during breaks. I play music to transition, instead of just a timer. I will say, "You have until the end of this song to finish this task. The song lasts 3 minutes and 52 seconds. Go." The urgency starts to build when the song is coming to an end. I use familiar enough songs that they will recognize when it is ending. This urgency works much like waiting until the night before something is due to get it done. Some of our best work comes out of pressure to finish on time.

You can create a mood with music. If you want people to feel calm, play classical music. If you want people to get excited, stick with party tunes. If you want people to flash back, go to the eighties and early nineties. Even if people were not born yet in those times, they know the music. Madonna, Michael Jackson, Whitney Houston, Miami Sound Machine, Def Leppard. The list goes on and on. My only suggestion is to think about your audience and adjust accordingly. Some songs work for anyone; but if you have a particularly young audience, you need to use music from today too. Meet people where they are and make them comfortable.

What can you do to evoke emotion in your learning experiences?

How can you get people to laugh with you, or if necessary, at you, to break the ice?

The next chapter walks you through my process for making sure people's emotions are tied to learning in my trainings. I make sure people feel valued, which, in my opinion, is the most important thing we can do for other humans, period; but it also happens to make learning stick.

# NEED TO KNOW

Use humor to break the ice. Let yourself laugh and find ways for others to laugh with you.

Be okay with a little silly. Claps and celebrations will help evoke the emotion that helps learning stick.

Use music to lighten the mood, smooth out transitions, and evoke emotion.

# NOTE-TAKING

What are two ways you are going to evoke emotion in your next training?

What do you need to do/practice to make those things happen?

# NEXT STEPS

Embrace the "cheese." It is okay to be cheesy to get a few laughs. Be willing to put yourself out of your comfort zone for the sake of your participants.

# Stickers

### MAKE LEARNING STICK

# NEED TO KNOW

- Understand the benefits of making participants feel valued and appreciated.
- Determine methods for doing so.

**TAKE NOTES**

Before shifting my career path to teach adults, I was a high school science teacher. I loved molding and shaping the minds of teenagers. High school is such an interesting time in life. In case you were unaware, between the ages of 14 and 18 humans actually know everything there is to know. Since they already know everything, educating this age group is quite a challenge.

Teenagers do not want or need to come to class because they, indeed, already know everything. This phenomenon stems back to a fear of appearing stupid. The students want to show those around them they have it all under control, but they have little to no control.

Guess what, adults are not much different. We all fear looking stupid in front of our peers. We want to show our bosses, colleagues, friends, and neighbors how smart we are. We avoid doing things that are difficult and cautiously approach learning opportunities with trepidation.

As a facilitator, you must break down those barriers if you want your participants to learn. You must create a space where vulnerability is safe and encouraged. It is your job to ease the minds of those in the room, replacing fear with safety. Although this sounds like a tall order, I have found an incredibly effective way to build trust quickly, so that learning can stick.

One day, I was in my classroom and I saw some stickers lying on my desk. I honestly have no idea what possessed me to pass them out, but I decided my seniors needed those stickers. I stood at the door of my portable (aka trailer because our school was overcrowded and I did not have a classroom in the building), stickers in hand, and proceeded to put a smiley face sticker on the hand of each student who walked into my room that afternoon.

The students' reactions to those stickers were remarkable. As I placed those stickers on their hands they smiled, they giggled, they showed their stickers to their friends, and they thanked me. Then, more miraculously, they sat down and were ready to learn. I remember that class feeling different. At the time, I did not understand why.

The next day, I had kind of forgotten about the stickers. The life of a high school teacher is a bit crazy, and I was simply not thinking about it. The first student came in and said, "Mrs. McMullen, where is my sticker?" My response to the first student was simply, "That was just a fluke idea yesterday; it wasn't meant to be a daily thing." But then the next student came in and asked too. They started saying things like, "We really liked them." "Can we get one every day?" "Please." High school students do not often say please unless it is important to them. I got out the stickers and started a pattern.

I told the students they had to show up on time to class to get a sticker. I taught in a portable in the very back of the school so students being tardy to class was a real struggle. I kid you not, I would have senior boys run from the cafeteria to my classroom for those stickers. I was dumbfounded. It was just a sticker. Or was it?

It did not take me long to realize it had very little to do with the sticker. One time I was busy putting grades in during class change, so I had a student stand at the door to pass out stickers for me; and the kids almost revolted. I discovered that day it was not about the sticker. It was about the physical and emotional interaction I had to have with each student to put that sticker on his or her hand. That simple act of authentic interaction showed them I cared about them. I noticed them. I loved them enough to say something individual to each one of them. It made them feel special.

My career shifted not long after that, and I went from having a classroom of my own to traveling to 35 schools in our district. I interacted with students who were not "my kids," and I saw them for only very short periods of time. I would guest teach or watch other teachers teach, and I had to build relationships in an instant. I decided to try my stickers again. I probably interacted with 10,000 students during those six years, and only 3 students ever turned down my stickers.

During those same six years I started teaching adults. On a whim, I decided to try using stickers with them too. I greeted them at the door before a training, asked them their names and gave them a sticker. I could not have predicted the reaction I got. Men and women alike loved the stickers. They would laugh and say it took them back to their childhood. After the initial sticker for showing up, to get stickers the participants had to share an idea, take a risk, or be a great learner. I have not ever seen people's hands shoot up to volunteer to answer questions like they do when there is a sticker involved.

A silent room teems with excitement with a simple phrase like, "What do you think? First three to respond get a chocolate scented sticker."

Without prompting, it became a competition to see who could earn the most stickers during a training. Sometimes, I would even give prizes to the person with the most stickers at the end of our learning time together. People eagerly dove into the learning. They worked together to gain more stickers, and they tied emotion to their learning as they instantly got rewarded for their efforts. I have now given stickers out across the nation, to superintendents, principals, teachers, students, colleagues, and friends. You are never too old for a sticker, because you are never too old to be valued.

It wasn't and never will be about the sticker. It was about being noticed, being celebrated, and being valued. The sticker was simply the vehicle that allowed me to break down barriers quickly and completely.

Ten years after I passed out my first sticker, one of my students from that class messaged me on Facebook. She said, "Mrs. McMullen, you will never guess what I found today. My sticker book." She had kept in a little book every sticker I had ever given her, and 10 years later still had that book. She told me it made her feel loved. Don't we all need just a little more love?

Just recently, I was teaching a masters' level course in Educational Leadership. Of course, I gave out stickers, because I really do not know how to function in a professional learning environment without them. There were six people in the course, and five of them absolutely loved stickers. One student wore them on her face every time she got one; another started a collection on his notebook.

One of the six, however, politely declined every time I offered her a sticker for something she had done well. I have been doing this too long to be deterred by her lack of desire for a sticker. I just simply asked her who she would like to give her sticker to, even though she was the one who earned it.

During our final class we talked about the leadership lessons we had learned and discussed over the 10-week course. We started talking about leverage, and how to get people to accept change even when it is hard. The stickers came up, and we discussed their purpose.

This woman, let's call her Tracy, was listening intently throughout the conversation. At the end, she took the floor. She said, "I know why I don't like the stickers." I was all ears, and we all leaned in to hear her answer. "I never received them as a child so there are no fond memories of them. More importantly, it stressed me out to decide where I am supposed to put them." "But," she added, "I think I see their value now. When trying to make people accept change, you have to meet them where they are. The stickers are meant to create instant leverage resulting in a higher likelihood of being accepting of the change. If I am being honest, I tried it with my students and they absolutely loved it."

Tracy brought stickers to her entire cohort and their new professor in term two of her master's program. She had a new understanding of the value of small gestures. She understood leverage.

Here's a little tip. Buy the smelly stickers. Everyone loves them the most. I have done years of research, trust me. They are a fan favorite.

Maybe you think a sticker is too cheesy or childish. That is totally okay. It is not natural for everyone to give stickers. It suits my personality. But remember, it is not about the sticker. It is about valuing your participants. So, if not a sticker, then what? How can you celebrate people in your trainings? What can you give them to make them not only want to participate, but want to open up to learning? Bragging rights can be motivation enough in many instances, but having something tangible can make all the difference.

Do you have swag for your organization? Could people earn time off, or money in the café, or a free coffee just for participating? Could there be a raffle for prizes at the end of a training?

It does not have to be expensive, but it does have to evoke value.

Learning can stick; whether it is a literal sticker or a figurative sticker, learning can stick. Be willing to be a bit unconventional, but only if it is authentic.

# NEED TO KNOW

Understand the benefits of making participants feel valued and appreciated. Determine methods for making participants feel valued and appreciated.

# NOTE-TAKING

Jot down a couple potential ways you will make your participants feel valued and appreciated. What changes might you see in the training outcomes if you employ this strategy?

# NEXT STEPS

Determine your sticker, and make it happen. Will it be a physical trinket or a kudos via email? Be sure whatever it is comes from the heart.

# Make Learning Memorable

In the last decade, I have trained roughly 2000 people in one capacity or another. Sometimes it was huge groups and other times small, intimate groups; but regardless of the number, I connected with my participants. I worked intentionally to make sure every person knew I cared.

Sometimes, I have the honor of getting to see the person I trained in action in their schools or places of business.

Years ago, I swore I would not go into a teacher's classroom without leaving a "nice note" on the desk or door, letting him or her know how much I loved what I saw. My thinking on this is simple, I want every teacher to know what he or she is doing is noticed.

This year, I got to go to a school I visited three years earlier. I even got to see some of the same teachers! When I got to this school, I was looking at all the great things on the wall, and I stopped short. I recognized my handwriting. There on the wall was the "nice note" I left in this teacher's classroom three years before. He had been in a training with me; then I got to see him in action, and my words mattered to him.

When learning is memorable, it will still make an impact years later. It will be worth remembering. It will contain nuggets of wisdom that translate and become a part of someone else's world.

While we were in his room, he started giving stickers to his students. I could not help smiling. I remembered giving him a sticker and he looked at me like I had grown a second head, at first. By the end of our learning time together, his hand always went up immediately so he could be the one to earn another sticker.

Now, three years later, he is giving stickers to his students; and they too were eager to share the right answers.

Learning needs to last; but it cannot do so if it is not first safe, logical, and fun. The memorable part comes when the other three are done well.

He knew I cared, he knew I approached things logically, and he knew I made it fun. Now, his students know the same thing about him.

Allowing learners to do the majority of the talking and holding them accountable for that conversation increases understanding and makes the learning last…because it was already safe, logical, and fun.

The goal of most learning opportunities is that the information be understood and utilized. Let's make sure that is true for you too.

Let's sing some *Summer Nights* and get everyone involved so it will last.

# Accountability

## MAKES LEARNING STICK

# NEED TO KNOW

- Build a plan.
- Spiral the learning.
- Assess understanding.

When I was in college, I had an accountability partner. Her name was Leslie; and I did not want to disappoint her, ever. Once a week we would meet and go through a list of 10 questions. We asked one another about our thoughts, our prayer life, or morality, and our overall well-being. Even though our meetings were on Tuesday nights, a day rarely passed without my thinking, "I better not do this because I am going to have to admit it to Leslie."

Leslie didn't judge me or make me feel bad for the things I did. Knowing I had to admit things to her simply kept me in check. When we know someone is going to be looking to see what we have or have not done, the chances of us doing those things increase.

Accountability comes in many different forms. Sometimes the facilitator can assist with accountability after the training ends; but more likely as the trainer, you will not be around to see if the participants use what they learned. However, you can help the leaders in the organization know what skills and behaviors to look for in their attendees as a result of the training. In fact, if you want learning to stick, one of the most important things you as the trainer can do is design an accountability system for using the new knowledge.

## HAVE A PLAN

We have already addressed how to plan for the training itself to run well. That plan is solid. Now you need to consider how you are going to create a plan with your participants so they will clearly see how to use the new information in their work and how they and their leadership can monitor use.

The action plan does not need to be terribly intense, but it does need to include some key components to ensure action takes place. Whether you are implementing this plan with the participants directly or the leadership team has given you the plan, it should include…

Creating a plan based on **who, what, when, where, how and why**.

WHO needs to be involved in the accountability system post training? Is it the leader of the department or organization or the attendees who went to the training, or both?

Once established, focus your plan on that group or groups. If you are working only with the participants, direct them to determine a good accountability partner in this work, perhaps someone who also attended the training or a partner back at work. If working with leadership, encourage them to create individual goals with staff and monitor progress toward those goals.

Create a template for the leadership with sample goals that include the performance objectives from the training. Knowing who needs to be involved in monitoring this work gives a solid foundation for sustaining the new behaviors/skills.

WHAT behaviors/skills do the participants need to perform differently or in addition to because of the training? Are there particular behaviors that need to change because of the training? What will have changed to show the participants/leadership that it is better? What are the 'look-fors?'

Create a sample checklist of the behaviors/skills covered in the training to be used as either observation or reflection instruments. These can be tailored to the audience identified in the 'Who.'

**WHEN** should the new practice be implemented? Help the participants/leadership set a timeline, and emphasize the importance of communicating the timeline to everyone involved.

Participants should post the timeline where they will be reminded. For leadership, make the discussion of the timeline and progress a regular part of one-on-one check-ins; and add it as a standing agenda item for meetings to keep it fresh in the minds of all involved.

**WHERE** in the workplace should results be seen? Are there tasks that should be more efficient due to the new practice? Should it take less time to complete something post training? Should fewer complaints come in about an event or way of work?

The where is a bit more results driven. Where could be a physical place, however it is more likely to be where in the workplace or situation the results will manifest.

**HOW** will you monitor this new way of work? How will the participants and/or the leadership utilize the checklist and/or provide feedback? The how should include a conversation with co-workers to determine the best new ways of work.

**WHY** do you want to implement this change? This is ultimately the most important question you can ask. Kotter suggests we create urgency when we want change to happen. The why for adults is specifically what can create that urgency. Why does the practice need to change? Why is this a value add for the organization? Why will this improve productivity? Why bother?

In an action plan it is important to allow the "why" to drive the who, what, when, where, and how. This portion of the action plan is likely filled with statements like, to better serve the clients with the product, or to get physically stronger.

Forbes recently produced an article titled, *The Wasted Dollars of Corporate Training Programs* that confirmed much of what we already know to be true. ***Training is only as good as the follow up.*** In 2018, the United States spent $87.6 BILLION on corporate training and development. That is a significant investment.

If we break it down, and take into consideration travel, personnel, lost time on the job for the personnel, etc., it would cost roughly $40,000 to train 30 people for one day. Yet, that training likely will not stick because $0 is spent on follow up. What if the company spent an additional $10,000 on follow up, whether it be a face-to-face regroup, a virtual survey or course, or a check in with the leaders in the organization about how the new learning is being incorporated into everyday life? For a quarter of the original cost, the learning will not have to be retaught. Most savvy business people would rather pay $50,000 resulting in a change in practice than $80,000 to train the same thing twice with no guarantees or monitoring of results.

If you are an external facilitator, leave the leaders of the organization with a follow-up plan. If you work within the company, work with your leaders in the organization to create a plan for monitoring the implementation of behaviors and skills and providing targeted follow up. Do not be a facilitator of a one-and-done experience.

Let's put this into context by walking through a plan.

**WHO:** Your data entry department is going to go to training to learn a new learning management system.

**WHAT:** Training happens January 5 and lasts for two days. The performance objective of the training is to provide participants the necessary skills to utilize a new learning management system (LMS) for the team. The old system is also going to be available to the team until June, with the expectation of a full implementation of the new LMS by June 1.

**WHEN:** Set two specific expectations for use by the beginning of February. Offer 15-minute refresher "how-to" videos on the use of those two expectations. Require all leaders to check in with their teams on the use of the new tools on February 1.

**WHERE & HOW:** February 1-15 monitor the use of the new expectations and reward with free lunch the team that is using only the new LMS. The manager will check on the team every Tuesday and Thursday to see if the new system is being utilized. If every team is using it exclusively, feed them all lunch, and celebrate the fact you transitioned long before your June 1 deadline. If you see those two have been fully adopted, go ahead and add another two.

**WHY:** What is measured matters! You must have ways to measure the things that you want to change in your organization. It is one thing to tell your staff members they need to do something, but it is something else entirely if you are checking to see that it is happening. Why do they need to use this new LMS system? It will improve productivity by 25% and streamline work for the entire department. The why is really determined by the leadership team prior to the training, but needs to be revisited with the people expected to execute the plan. This will keep the relevance fresh in the minds of those who need to use the new way of work.

It is necessary to make the change a requirement that is monitored, and then support your people in making the change attainable.

- Offer the type(s) of support needed to make the change safe.
- Celebrate those who adopt the new change well.
- Monitor whether the change is being implemented.
- Re-train when necessary.

## ASSESSMENT OF UNDERSTANDING

Check-ins throughout the training experience will help you know which direction to head with the next segment.

Check-ins can be brief and will be powerful. One of the easiest ways to check in with your participants is to simply ask how they are feeling about a concept. The problem with this method is most adults are not comfortable admitting in a room full of their peers they do not understand something. If you make the sharing anonymous you are more likely to get authentic answers.

Have everyone grab two post-it notes before break. On one write something learned during the last hour, and on the other write something confusing or uncertain about the content. Place them on either side of a poster in the back on the way out for break. This simple gesture will very quickly tell you two things. It will tell you what point or points you covered well. Those will be the ones under the "What did you learn?" side of the poster. The confusing or uncertain column will tell you what you might want to revisit right after the break. I know you have a tight schedule, but if over half the room is struggling with the same concept, the concept is worth revisiting. Be realistic though. If one or two people are struggling with something, the entire group does not need to go back over that subject.

Another easy way to assess the understanding in the room is to have the participants hold up a number 0-5 showing their comfort level with the topic. It is telling to do this one before you present a topic and again after the topic is complete. Have the participants hold their hand close to their chest so they do not feel judged. Scan the room and look for growth. You might not get everyone to a five in the short time you have with them; but if you can show movement along the continuum, you are doing something right.

## A SPIRALED LEARNING APPROACH

*Accountability is key*, and as the facilitator you do not always have the ability to hold people accountable after they leave your training. You do, however, always have the opportunity to embed accountability in your training. Therefore, you need to structure your training to spiral the learning to build in accountability.

Even if you do not have direct opportunities to be involved in the follow-up monitoring of your participants and their utilization of the training content, there are ways you can still reinforce the training objectives after the training has ended.

Your goal is not only to help people have a successful and enjoyable experience with you, but also that the performance objectives are met, internalized, and later utilized by the attendees. Yet, you realize when presenting information there needs to be some space and time for the learning to be absorbed. If the participants hear the information once, and only read it, they will not remember it as well as if they do something with that information.

*There is a formula to burn information into someone's brain.*
*Sprinkle. Splash. Flood. Drip. Drip. Drip.*

I attended a training fourteen years ago, and this is what stuck. The training was for teachers by a company called Performance Excellence for All Kids (PEAK), and we were learning how to introduce new material in a scaffolded and spiraled way. That is 'teacher speak' for layered and revisited. If you have a cumulative test at the end of a course, the expectation is you remember what you learned at the beginning of the course just as well as you remember what you learned at the end.

## LET'S TRANSLATE THIS INTO TRAINING

The analogy works for me because I live in Florida, where rain is quite the experience. I have seen it rain sideways for five solid minutes and then stop completely, leaving one side of the road completely dry. The problem with a hard rain, however, is much of the water is lost in runoff.

If I were going to describe the rain in Florida, I would say it sprinkles, then splashes a bit, then floods, and finally drip, drip, drips. The rain does not fall the same way throughout the storm.

The same theory holds true when delivering information. If you do not give ample time for the information to sink in and be revisited, most of it will be lost in "runoff."

This is a teaser to the main event. Think about the first time you hear about a new movie. It is not the actual trailer, but it does make you excited about what is to come. In professional learning, this could be a flier about an upcoming training, or an email letting the team know of an opportunity for learning.

This is the preview to the movie. You find out more about what to expect and you have a better understanding of the purpose behind the training. In professional learning, this is the blurb you explain at a team meeting, or a follow-up email giving more details about a training, complete with expectations.

This is the movie. This is your training. You give the bulk of the information during this time. This is the professional learning opportunity. This can be anywhere from one hour to several days in length. The flood is where the bulk of the learning takes place. New concepts and skills are presented and discussed.

In an actual flood, all the water cannot be absorbed because it comes too fast for the soil. Much of the water is lost in run off. The same is true during professional learning. There may be many concepts presented during a professional learning opportunity and much of it may be new to the learner. The learning runoff needs to be captured in a reservoir for later use.

This is the most often forgotten and yet most valuable way to keep people talking about the learning. This is the idea that a sequel is coming or a critique of the film. In training, these are reminders of key points in the training. The drips force people to think about what they learned during the flood.

As I just mentioned, I live in Florida, where it rains with passion and fervor. Right after the rain, the trees begin to drip. Because it is so humid, sometimes the dripping can last for a full day after the rain stops. In training, the dripping needs to last for weeks or months. The learners may not be ready to absorb the learning until weeks later when they had time to think through the topics individually. They didn't need the information yet.

Revisiting concepts a week after, two weeks after, a month later reinforces the learning. These are reminders of the great learning that happened during the flood. There should be a component of the drip requiring action. Maybe it is an email response, or a quick activity that can be done with a colleague. These drips take theory into action for the learner. Without them, the learning may not be operationalized, but instead be forgotten or remain just theory without action.

My husband works for an organization that uses Salesforce. Salesforce is a brilliant organizational tool that can tell you almost anything you want to know about any potential client in the world. It will store conversations, link data, and do Calculus while making you a cup of tea, IF you know how to use it.

His company received training once on how to use Salesforce. Unfortunately, because there has not been ongoing training, or any accountability the sales team is using it, none of the awesome features it can do are being used. They are using basic spreadsheets and emails because that is more comfortable. No one is forcing them to use the very best tool that exists for their work.

*There was no drip,*

*drip,*

*drip.*

What if instead of a one-time training, the sales team had been exposed to Salesforce features once a week for a month. Each time the challenge for the week would be to use the new feature with at least one client. At the next training, the team would share how that feature worked and what was good or bad about it. The next week a new feature would be added. Even though they may not need all the features in that particular month, the accountability and reminders would help the sales team look for reasons to use it. The dripping would remind the team and the result would be an increased use of the features of Salesforce.

Now that you have a better understanding of the *Sprinkle, Splash, Flood, Drip, Drip, Drip* concept, how do you see that relating to accountability and follow up?

If you incorporated the revisiting of training objectives with your participants to reinforce concepts and provide opportunity for follow up, how would participant outcomes be altered?

Have you participated in professional learning where the facilitator intentionally created opportunities for follow up? Can you see yourself incorporating that technique in your training?

What follow-up opportunities can you provide to help refresh their memories of the learning?

What assessment tools do you have that will let you know whether your audience understood the content or not?

How might you assist in creating a plan for follow-up monitoring of the implementation of training objectives?

# NEED TO KNOW

Build a plan, either for the participants, with the participants, or with the leadership team. Regardless, build a plan for follow up and accountability. Spiral the learning so topics are revisited more than once.
Assess understanding throughout the process.

# NOTE-TAKING

Write down specific ways you are going to know if your participants understood the content. How will you create the drip, drip, drip?

# NEXT STEPS

Find creative ways, both during and after your training, to hold people accountable for what they learned. Build an accountability plan that covers who, what, when, where, how, and why.

# Talking

## MAKES LEARNING STICK

# NEED TO KNOW

- Remember the person talking is the person learning.
- Make sure participants are exhausted.
- Use simple tools.

The person doing the talking is the person doing the learning. Once a facilitator of adult learners understands this fact, everything about the learning opportunity changes.

I once attended a training conducted by the department of education. The trainer read to us directly from the PowerPoint presentation for six straight hours! Not one single inflection of the voice, or expression in the tone, just painful reading. I was there for six hours and not once had the chance to utter a word. You may not be able to tell by reading, but I am 100% extrovert. I need to talk to process. Painful does not begin to describe it.

As a facilitator, particularly when you are brought in as an expert, the natural tendency is to tell those in your audience everything they need to know.

Here's the problem. You now know this information much better than you did when you started, and everyone in the room only grabbed a small fraction of what you said. Participants need to be the ones doing the talking and learning. You are the expert right now; but by the time they leave your session, they should be well on their way to being experts too.

There is a very simple rule for sharing information; for every ten minutes of information shared, whether it is a video, lecture, or demonstration, there should be two minutes of processing and two minutes of discussion. The processing might be done independently. The processing could be written or in the participant's head. Regardless of how it happens, the processing must happen. The discussion, which happens immediately after the processing, solidifies the understanding for all the participants.

As the professional learning facilitator, this break in the delivery of information will not happen naturally. You will have to write it into your notes to stop and let the participants talk. It might help to set a timer as a reminder to stop talking every ten minutes or so. Or maybe you determine where a natural break might fall in the material you are sharing. Regardless, you must let people chew on the material on their own.

The goal is for the participants to wrestle with the information, not the facilitator. Every training was designed to teach the participants something. Unfortunately, without this processing time, the facilitator will end up leaving with the bulk of the knowledge. There are some specific ways to shift the focus back where it belongs.

The number one question I ask myself when facilitating a training is, "Am I saying something the participants could be saying instead?" If the answer is yes, I find a way to pass the baton back to them. It is not that I do not have any knowledge to share. It is, instead, when the participants are able to read some information then discuss it, or discuss it after hearing me share with them, that the learning becomes solidified.

So often, and I was guilty of this too, a trainer thinks he or she must say every new piece of information for the participants to understand it. That simply is not true. The participants often already hold great knowledge in the topics. Remember to honor the brilliance in the room. If the topic is new, they will retain more of it if given the opportunity to talk about it with their colleagues, instead of just listening.

I could stand in front of you and tell you all about how to create reports in Salesforce. I could show you what to do, have guides for how to do it, tell you all the great things this tool will do to enhance your work; but if I don't involve you in the learning, only I learned more about Salesforce.

What if, instead, I gave you a "one-pager" of directions for using Salesforce, asked you to read it and mark the things you do and do not understand, then let you talk with a partner or in a triad, and gave you time to explore? Once you have had some time to explore the learning, I bring you back together as a whole group so that questions that could not be figured out could be addressed. How would this shift the understanding and buy in from your participants?

What if, instead of sharing the ten ways to improve your sales techniques, you had the group watch a short video of someone on a sales call and then critique what was seen using a list of techniques and definitions as a guide? Once the room had identified the techniques, then they could role play the scenarios themselves with a partner, using those same techniques. The participant needs to be doing the heavy lifting.

Let's talk weight-lifting for a second. I love going to bootcamp. I have been going for seven years at 5:15 am. I realize that is an ungodly hour; but to me, it is worth it. I like getting stronger and pushing myself beyond what I thought I could do.

Weightlifting, however, truly benefits only the person with the weights in her hands. If I stand in front of you and do bicep curls while telling you how you should lift weights, my arms will get stronger and yours will not benefit one bit. Frequently in a training session, the facilitator does all the heavy lifting. I can pump iron while telling you all the right techniques, which weights you should choose, and how imperative it is to bend your knees; but I am still the one reaping the majority of the benefit.

Instead of you watching me lift weights, I have to put the weights into your hands, spot you if and when necessary, adjust the amount of weight to meet your needs and coach you through the exercise. Then you reap the benefit! As a facilitator, this is true every single time. It is time to teach your participants to lift weights rather than performing for them.

I, as the facilitator, am not the one doing the talking. I am simply guiding the learning. If I am exhausted at the end of the training because I did all the heavy lifting, and my participants are well-rested because they took a little nap at their tables after lunch, the wrong person did all the learning.

How can you ensure your participants are the ones who are lifting the weights in your trainings?

What do you do if you realize you are doing all the heavy lifting? How can you transfer responsibility?

WRITE YOUR THOUGHTS HERE:

## CLEAR DIRECTIONS

We waste precious time during trainings because we give directions, assume participants understand what is being asked of them and turn them loose. Inevitably, the next five minutes of a 10-minute activity is spent trying to figure out what is supposed to be done. It is possible to avoid this issue altogether though. It just takes some intentional practices.

After you give directions, ask the participants to repeat the directions "better than I just did" to a partner at the table. They are repeating the directions to a partner and working through what they both remembered. This will allow those who were listening to share their expertise and will catch the person up who may have missed the directions. This will eliminate wasted time.

In every training room there are three types of participants. The first type cannot wait to learn. These people choose to sit in the front, take notes without being asked, and always catch the directions the first time. The second type listens but can get easily distracted. They catch about half of the information the first time around but can fake their way through most things. The third type does not want to be there at all. These people are likely on their phones or zoning out the majority of the time. When you ask people to repeat the directions, you are honoring all three types of learners.

Type one is so excited, you are not having to explain a second or third time. Now it is their turn to shine and share expertise. Type two is also honored in this activity. These participants are forced to be a little more focused the next time, because they know it will pay off. The third type gets to be told a second time what the expectations are without having to ask. This is true of your children as well. Seek clarity of understanding from them before releasing them to do a task. It solidifies the learning.

## TOOLS FOR READING

Give people tools for reading. The goal when reading information is to retain it; but without tools, that is often a tall order. I suggest something simple like question marks and exclamation points. A question mark signifies something confusing in the text or something that makes you curious. An exclamation point indicates an idea you like or agree is helpful.

Ask the participants to read the one pager I mentioned earlier in this chapter about tips for using Salesforce; but as they read, use question marks and exclamation points to mark their understanding and learning. Once they are done reading and marking the text, you can have the table discuss the question marks as a group and try to come up with answers to the questions. You can also have them share the exclamation points and discuss how this information fits into their daily work. Discussion after reading helps make the information more digestible and helpful.

Speaking of reading, another important thing to remember is to never read something to a room of learners when they can read it for themselves. Allow the participants to read on their own the material you wish to cover. In the education world, we call this a flipped classroom. It is flipped because the reading happens at home, and the question asking and learning happens while you are together. We let the independent work, also known as "prework," cover new topics. What if you asked your participants to read new information before they came to the training? How would this help maximize the learning time you have together?

If you are worried people will come unprepared, build in a little time at the beginning of the training to let them review the information one more time. Those who did it at home will have it fresh in their heads, and those who did not will be able to grab a couple nuggets of wisdom.

Because they read the material prior to coming together, when the group is physically together, they can wrestle with how to incorporate what was learned into their workspace, instead of hearing the information for the first time in the training. Utilizing a pre-read allows for a deeper dive into the information. A deeper dive will more likely yield better implementation of the new skill, product or idea.

When it is time to share the information being processed, avoid one person dominating the information sharing. Instead of asking the entire room what they think—yielding one or two people answering the question— have each table share ideas with one another or have everyone share with a partner. This technique multiplies the brilliance in the room, again increasing the number of people leaving with useful and applicable understanding of the information.

It is also valuable, when learning new information, to present that information in digestible chunks. As mentioned, our brains file information based on where we were when we learned it. If we learn everything while sitting in the same spot in the room, our brain creates one large file, which we have to sift through to pull up any of that information. If participants move around the room while learning information, a new file is created in the mind. It is easier to find information when it is organized in several files rather than one large one. Getting participants up and moving will help them chunk and retain information.

Drip. Drip. Drip.

# NEED TO KNOW

Remember the person doing the talking is the person doing the learning.

Let the participants do the majority of the talking while you facilitate the learning.

Make sure the participants are the ones who are exhausted at the end of the training, because they did all the heavy lifting.

Use simple tools when reading to help the learning jump off the page.

# NOTE-TAKING

What techniques will you use to make sure that the participants are doing the bulk of the talking?

# NEXT STEPS

Find ways to put the weights in the hands of your participants if you want the learning to last.

# Can Virtual Learning Stick?

## NEED TO KNOW

- Create norms for virtual learning.
- Call people by name.
- Use breakout rooms and the chat.

COVID-19 brought with it a brand-new set of challenges for just about every facet of life. Suddenly, kindergarteners were Zooming with their classmates, grandparents were hosting virtual happy hours, and businesses switched to "work-from-home" models. Some people transitioned beautifully, but other transitions were not so smooth.

I have worked from home for the last seven years, so this was not a brand-new world for me. I work for an organization of about 250 employees of which roughly 150 work in an office building. In March of 2020, those employees got the opportunity to join the rest of us in our virtual world. We got to see inside people's homes, meet their children and pets, and navigate new waters together.

For four years, I have sent a daily motivational email to about 80 women in my organization to remind them that they are loved and worthy. I often shared workouts or recipes with them, and we would do a 30-day challenge every month to improve ourselves. When we would be together for events, I would host a bootcamp at the hotel so we could actually work out together. It was always such a blessing.

Once we all had to be home, I decided to host a 30-minute virtual workout with the women I had been encouraging online for years. I have a faithful few who have not missed a workout; but what blows my mind is how many of these women are watching the recordings and doing the workouts in their own time zones on their own time, asynchronously.

I have connected with women that I have only ever met in a virtual space; and we have sweated together, laughed together, and become better together.

Virtual learning can be every bit as impactful as a face-to-face experience. It is all about delivery and technique.

Learning and training should not stop just because we cannot physically be together, but there is a right and a wrong way to conduct this type of training.

The overall themes are the same as with a face-to-face training, but there are nuances to keep in mind.

Training in the virtual realm often has a negative connotation, likely because of the painfully boring webinars produced by some organizations. There is no life or excitement in the voice of the presenter. There is absolutely no interaction between the presenter and the participants. Never is a participant asked to participate actively. These types of trainings remind me of watching paint dry, boring as sin and not particularly productive. They are conducted by the "Bueller" teacher of the 2000's.

Virtual learning does NOT have to be that way. It can be interactive, insightful, and fun. The trainer needs to set the stage for the learning space, use the great tools available, and be present.

Virtual trainings can be either synchronous or asynchronous. Synchronous trainings happen in live time. Everyone attends the training at the same time. The presenter is live and all interaction happens simultaneously. My workouts can be done synchronously, and different women join me all the time.

Asynchronous trainings happen at the leisure of the user. These are often courses built into a learning management system and are designed for the participants to work at their own pace. This happens when my friends click on the recording link and do the workout on their own.

I am an adjunct professor at National Louis University for the Tampa campus. Most of our courses used to be taught face to face; but recently, pre-COVID, we decided to try a virtual cohort. At first, everyone was concerned it would not be as personal as our face-to-face sessions; but the demand was there, so we wanted to give it a shot. I taught the students for their second term, and I knew after the first night this was going to be one of the best learning experiences ever. I conducted those classes from multiple airports, hotel rooms, and my home office. We would play, "Where in the world is Christie McMullen?" at the beginning of every class.

I never had to miss a class because of my work travel schedule, and we could have meaningful interactions regardless of my venue. More importantly than convenience for me, the students bonded beautifully. They did not have the stress of driving through traffic to attend class. They were in the comfort of their own homes. They were able to look everyone in the eye at the same time using gallery view on Zoom. They relied on one another to find answers. They were a team.

After we all moved to our "home offices" when the pandemic hit, much of America was forced to find their way in this new space of virtual learning. The positive experience I had with my virtual master's cohort can be the norm for training experiences as well.

The key to a successful virtual experience includes everything from the book to date with some increased accountability and relevance. You will need to make sure the participants are tracking with you by doing additional check ins. You should read your audience just as you would face to face. The virtual space does not have to be scary; it just has to be nuanced.

## NORMS

Set specific parameters for the meeting time that are clear from the beginning. As discussed in the structure section, you set the tone for the training; and you determine what is and is not acceptable. It works best when the participants also buy into your expectations, which can be done by giving them space to explore the norms and agree or disagree to them.

Very seldom do people disagree with norms, but you may end up tweaking them for your audience. When that audience is a virtual one, some things need to be non-negotiable; but you should still present that with flexibility.

For example, cameras should be on. Period. With large groups, they may be turned off to limit distracted .. ? periodically create options for a few people to turn them back on. If a camera is turned off it is temporary, to handle a specific situation; and otherwise we are all in this together. Devices should be muted unless you are speaking. Positive intent should be assumed when reading chats or posts.

Another important norm in virtual space is to assume positive intent and frame answers to do so as well. Words in a chat are much like words in an email. Tone is left up to interpretation. Help participants understand the culture of your virtual training is an uplifting one.

Think about what norms should be set to ensure a successful training. Jot them down here.

WRITE YOUR THOUGHTS HERE:

## EXPLORE THE PLATFORM

Zoom, Microsoft Teams, Big Blue Button, GoTo Meeting, Google Hangout, WebEx, the list goes on and on. Each platform does the same thing—creates a space for groups of people to meet and collaborate. Even if you are very familiar with one platform, if you are asked to navigate a different platform things just are not the same.

Take a few moments at the beginning of the meeting to allow participants to play with the new features. Have a screen shot guide page of the features you will be using, then let them try those features. If you are going to use emojis, ask them to add one to the chat that signifies how they are feeling today. If you want them to see one another, show them how to expand the view to see more than the speaker. If you want them to "raise their hand" to be acknowledged, show them how.

Do not assume that everyone knows where these features are. These two minutes of explicit instruction on the features of the platform will increase your engagement exponentially. Use the platform's website to learn what it can do. They all have how-to videos ready for you to use. Use the tools that already exist to make your learning experience even better.

## NAMES

Names are listed under the participants' pictures, so use them. Call people by name. This action makes them feel more connected and noticed, which makes checking out a more difficult option. Make eye contact with each person intentionally. If they don't have their camera on, focus on your camera when you are speaking so it will feel like you are speaking directly to them.

Encourage participants to call one another by name as well. There are really no excuses not to do so, since their names are neatly labeled under their pictures, but you set the tone.

Greet them when they "enter the virtual room" just like you would if they were entering a training room. Make them feel welcome by calling each person by name and asking for something good that is going on in his/her world to be added to the chat box. Involving them from the beginning will set the stage for a collaborative time together.

It is easy to change your name on some platforms, so know that if the screen says something like "reconnecting" or "poor connection" that just means a tech savvy participant is choosing to check out.

## CAMERAS

Turn. Them. On.

Give your participants warning that the expectation is for cameras to be on during the training. Everyone appreciates that heads up so hair is brushed and shirts are appropriate.

Set the tone by having yours on from the beginning. As people join, encourage them to turn theirs on as well. Sometimes bandwidth can be an issue, but most of the time, it works great.

If you have more than one monitor, notice where your camera is and do your best to keep your eyes on that screen when speaking. If you have to look at another monitor, let the participants know why you are looking away. You do not want to appear as though you are not paying attention when in reality you are intently staring at the content.

In addition to having your camera on, share your screen when appropriate. Show people what you are discussing. Visuals make a world of difference when trying to get participants to understand something. Show them rather than just telling them what you are discussing.

Be careful, though, because some people forget that their cameras are on and embarrassing situations happen. I participated in a doctoral webinar once that all master's students were required to attend. One of the participants did not realize her camera was on. She started out sitting up, then she grabbed a blanket and slowly laid down. Within five minutes she had her eyes closed and was sound asleep, on camera, in front of all her professors and her peers. What I want to know is why didn't a friend text her to say, "Um, you might want to turn your camera off!" It made for some great pictures for me though!

## BREAKOUT ROOMS

If the training were held face to face, participants should talk to one another in a variety of groupings. Sometimes in partners, sometimes trios, sometimes table groups, and often with new faces. The same is absolutely true in a virtual setting. Let them talk to one another.

Breakout rooms are easy to use. Not every platform allows them, but a back-channel chat can be done regardless of platform. This is just a side meeting that happens during the main meeting.

If for some reason breakout rooms are not an option, use the chat option often. Ask a question then have participants put their responses into the chat and respond to everyone. You can then choose to share a couple or ask a few participants to expand upon their answer.

## CHATS

After asking a group question, let the participants put their individual answers in the chat. This will increase the number of people thinking about and answering the question. You are also able to hold everyone accountable by looking for names and responses. Having the answers posted will increase understanding by all participants as well, as long as you encourage people to read what other people wrote.

Talk about what people wrote, but don't feel the need to read every response. Look for a response or two that would spark good conversation or drive a specific point home for you and share that one. Be strategic in which one you select. Bring in participants who have been quiet or reluctant to share. This will spread and share the brilliance in the room.

Public chats are different from private chats, and not every platform allows for both. Let participants know the difference so you can avoid inappropriate statements coming to everyone. You do not all need to know that Chloe and Sabrina have dinner plans for tomorrow night.

## MICROPHONES

Let. Them. Talk.

I realize when there are 200 people on a video chat, microphones need to be muted for control purposes. Barking dogs and crying babies make it hard for everyone to focus. However, if your voice is the only one heard for an entire presentation, guess who learned something in the presentation: YOU! You must engage your audience and vary the voices in the room. Ask questions, then ask people to use the raise your hand feature; and you can call on individuals. You can even just unmute them when it is their turn to speak. Don't be afraid to share control. What you are really sharing is the opportunities to learn.

Of course, there will be some mishaps, but the benefit far outweighs the cost of controlling contributions. I ate an entire salad with my camera off and my microphone on during a team meeting. Finally, someone said, "Christie, is it good?" Oops. That is still better than never letting people speak. And as the presenter, you can mute individuals if need be.

## OPPORTUNITIES

As with any new situation, everything will not go smoothly every time. Look at the mishaps as opportunities for growth. If someone is having their lawn mowed and no one can hear anything else, learn how to mute others before the next session. If no one turned on the camera, think about ways to make it safe to be seen and set the culture to do so next time. Laugh when things go poorly. Find the bright spots.

A bright spot is something that is going well. As humans, we tend to focus on the dark spots, or the things that are not going as well. Focusing on bright spots allows for light to shine on the surrounding areas as well. You can choose to focus on the positive or the negative; both are there. The one you choose to focus on will determine your overall outlook. Choose wisely.

All the other rules from previous chapters still apply.

# MAKE IT

*safe logical fun memorable*

Who is talking? Who is doing the heavy lifting? What is the accountability plan? How will you know they learned it? What follow up will take place to ensure learning?

Just because you are not face to face with the participants does not mean you cannot engage with them in a thoughtful and productive way. Use all the things you learned in this book and couple them with all the amazing things you already do as a trainer; trust they will work in a virtual space as well.

We are all learning to navigate this space together, but it can be an incredibly effective space if you allow it to be.

# NEED TO KNOW

Create norms for virtual learning, which is ultimately a plan for success. Call people by name and make them feel welcome, using cameras to increase involvement and the feeling of belonging.

Use breakout rooms and the chat feature to foster rich conversation, turning on microphones and letting the people talk!

# NOTE-TAKING

What will you do in the virtual space to make the learning feel as personal as it does in the physical realm? How will you involve participants actively in the learning?

# NEXT STEPS

Be bold and brave. This is not the same as face-to-face interaction, but it can be every bit as effective. Give yourself a little grace as you work through the kinks of a new platform, then embrace the learning opportunity for what it is.

# Learning Stuck, Now What?

## NEED TO KNOW

- Revisit the "need to knows."
- Determine next steps.
- Create a follow-up opportunity.
- Reflect on the experience personally.

In the spirit of old movie references, the "Stay at Home" order for COVID-19 made every day feel like *Groundhog Day*. Get up, work hard, stay home, repeat. We were forced to slow down and be still. We were given the gift of time to process and use what we learned to do things differently.

Some of us built new habits that were positive ones. Exercise, meditation, quiet time, spending quality time with family. Other habits were not so positive. For example, my cousin said she had to take a nap to force herself to stop snacking! And I am pretty sure drinking nightly should not be the norm. But guess what, the learning we did during COVID -19 will likely stick. We **repeated** it, we **reflected** on it, we **thought** about it, and we executed new ways of work. Good and bad.

The only way these new ways of work you learned in this book will stick is if you do the same.

**Repeat** the ideas in your head. **Reflect** on what you learned. **Think** about the different components of the techniques and execute new ways of work.

When the ban lifts, we will be a little more cognizant of dirty surfaces, and that is a good thing. We will recognize the value of quality time with family, again a good thing. Because we were fully immersed in this new way of life, the learning will be sticky.

When you close this book, you will only take with you what you choose to use. It will not go perfectly the first time, but it will get better with time.

You will change the learning experience to be safe, logical, fun, and memorable or you will at least tackle one idea at a time.

But, now what?

Perhaps the most valuable part of the training happens after the day is done.

# REVISIT THE "NEED TO KNOW" OBJECTIVES

What did you set out to do with this training? Meeting? Conversation?

Did the objectives get accomplished? Were they on point for what you wanted the training to do? Do those objectives need to be altered to better serve the needs of participants in the future?

You can and should ask this question at the end of the training, but you should also reach back out a few weeks after the training is over to see how implementation is going. This could be a simple email with the objectives listed and the question, "How is it going and how can I help?"

It could be to survey the participants a month or so after the training, asking about the objectives, specifically, and how implementation is going. This could be done with a survey or a phone call. It might look like this.

**Objective:** Participants will utilize a new Learning Management System when working with new clients.

**Survey Question:** On a scale of 1-5, five being all the time and one being never, please answer the following question. I use the new Learning Management System when working with new clients… 1 2 3 4 5

You can share this type of information with leadership teams to determine if more training is needed or if more accountability is necessary. You can also use this information to tweak your future trainings. What stuck? What did not? What gaps do you need to fill next time you present this information?

The survey should not be more than five questions and should be quick to complete. Do yourself a favor and use multiple choice responses whenever possible. Open ended questions are less likely to be completed and require you to work much harder to analyze the data. Likert scales work well to determine the range of implementation.

What if the learning opportunity was an in-office meeting conducted by a manager? Is a survey the best option? Maybe an email follow-up with the team would be sufficient in this case. Or maybe this topic warrants a chance to discuss things further in an open online forum. You know your people and their needs, just choose to be aware enough of them to do something to support their needs.

## DETERMINE NEXT STEPS WITH THE LEADERS OF THE ORGANIZATION

Last year I got to conduct a training with about 25 medical field workers ranging from floor nurses to dental hygienists, to front office managers. These

amazing men and women were in my session because they needed to know how to get other people to learn, and they were not yet sure how. They had been selected as trainers because they were the best in their field. That meant that they knew everything about the content but had not yet been trained in how to get other people to understand the content.

One lady asked me how to get the floor nurses she was training to remember how to fill out the forms properly for discharging patients.  After doing some digging, I discovered that every time she showed her nurses how to complete the form, she was the one holding the pen.  We talked about shifting the weights into the hands of the new nurses, so they were the ones with the knowledge.

I circled back with that nurse about 30 days later, and she was so excited to report that her nurses were now completing the discharge forms properly. I asked her what else she needed from me; and because she had success with the first learning opportunity, she asked me to share another.  The feedback she gave me also included the fact that she needed a refresher about two weeks after our session.  I needed that feedback and would not have gotten it if I had not asked.

Ideally this type of plan for revisiting is done before the training ever starts, but it is also important to revisit these ideas once the training ends.  Be proactive and ask for this meeting in advance.  The more you know about where the organization is heading, the better you will be able to steer the ship in that direction.

Reach out a month or so after delivering the training to see how things are going and if they need a review.  This will increase your credibility and add to the learning from the participants.  Offer to support the team by doing a follow up one-hour question and answer session, or a virtual refresher that could be done synchronously or asynchronously.  Simply offer support and ask how implementation is going.

Use the survey that you gave to participants to spark deeper conversations about next steps and ideas for moving forward.  You know exactly what the participants adopted and what they ignored.  You revisited the objectives that the leadership team helped to build, so you can also solve the issue of gaps in implementation.

Offer solutions to fill the gaps. Gaps are going to show up, but you can offer to fill those gaps. Know their data before you talk to them; offer opportunities to continue the learning and fill the needs of the participants, or patients, or students, or children.

## GATHER FEEDBACK SO YOU CAN GET BETTER NEXT TIME

At the end of every training you should offer space for the participants to leave feedback. It can be as simple as three questions.

*What are three things you learned from this training?*
*What is one thing you need more support to embrace or understand?*
*What can I do to improve the facilitation next time?*

If you ask these questions you will know:

1. What stuck with the majority of the audience?
2. What wasn't as sticky or harder to absorb by the majority?
3. What needs to be done to hone my craft?

When analyzing these data, be sure to dismiss the true outliers. We often fixate on the one person who did not have a good experience instead of noticing the 32 people who did have a great experience. I am not saying to ignore the outliers all together, because they contain that person's truth; but you cannot dwell on the one or two. Focus on the majority and learn from the minority.

I once conducted a training that ended with a giant group hug. There was that much bonding and camaraderie in the room. When I read through the evaluations they were glowing. "Best training I have ever attended." "I learned more today than I have in the last year." "So much learning and fun." And then I found one that said, "Next time, have more chocolate." Really?! More chocolate? Why did that person bother saying anything at all?

I was frustrated because it would have been a perfect record of happy participants, but this person screwed it up. Or did he? His needs were not quite met. He was satisfied with the learning, but his belly wasn't satisfied. We can't learn when our basic needs of food, water, shelter, and chocolate are not met. I did not let the comment derail my excitement for a good training, but I did let it guide my candy purchase the next time.

Outliers are just that, anomalies. You can notice them, and maybe even adjust something minor, but you should not ignore the majority. Overall, what did people think? Did they get something out of the training? Was the something they got the something you intended for them to get?

If most of the group had a positive experience that ended with a better understanding of the material, then do not change a thing. If they missed major points, or fixated on the wrong things, adjust accordingly. Feedback is meant to help you become better. Don't take it personally, but take it.

You will get better with every single presentation if you learn from every single presentation. Be willing to grow and evolve as you multiply your audience.

## CREATE A FOLLOW-UP OPTION THAT ALLOWS FOR A REFRESHER

My nurse friend needed a follow up, and I was not there to give it. What if I had set up an opportunity for her to keep learning without me?

Think virtual and self-guided. You do not have to be the one to deliver the follow up, nor does it have to happen live; but it does need to happen. How can you create space for the learning to continue after you leave? What

types of questions would prompt learning and growth? Can you make it happen or should the organization do so themselves? I don't care how it happens; I care that it happens! Make it happen. You will save time and money if you can make this a virtual experience.

Our world looks a little different than it ever has. Much of our training is transitioning to the online world, as will our follow up. Travel does not feel as safe, yet. Budgets have been slashed; therefore travel cannot happen, even if it does feel safe. Find ways to connect that does not involve being in the same place at the same time.

The virtual world can be synchronous or asynchronous, and both have advantages. Synchronous requires everyone to be together at the same time, creating constraints when trying to run an organization. Synchronous also allows for synergy and relationship building. It gives space for the participants to interact and learn from one another at the same time.

Asynchronous learning does not involve live interaction, but it can involve untimed interactions. Discussion posts and blog type entries, read by others, allow for learning to happen when it is convenient for the learner. Asynchronous lets learning take place after hours, before hours, during hours, and in stolen moments. If I have 15 minutes, I can do 15 minutes of a module. I do not have to wait until I have a three-hour chunk of time.

Your follow up should be a combination of both asynchronous, self-guided learning and synchronous, facilitator-guided learning. It absolutely can be face to face; but just know that if that is not an option, virtual certainly is.

Do not be afraid of virtual learning. Some people feel it is less personal, but I totally disagree. As I said before, I have been an adjunct professor for the last several years. Most of my courses have been taught face to face, but my most recent cohort was completely virtual. I can honestly say that I had more personal interactions and a tighter bond with my virtual group than any other I have ever had. I took the time to build relationships, cameras on, with my students, and we nurtured those relationships every time we were together. I believe they were a stronger cohort because they had to rely on one another and trust that the technology would work.

Learning does not fit in a box; it instead lives in every experience we have. As facilitators, we must create a space where the learning can be continuous and safe. Follow-up learning follows the same rules. Find a way to carry those relationships you built during your training time into the months and even years to follow.

## REFLECT ON YOUR EXPERIENCE

Reflection is mission critical. If you do not look back on how things went, you will be destined to repeat the same mistakes every single time. Beyonce is an amazing performer, no doubt, but do you know what helps make her that way? She films every single performance, and that night, after the lights are off and the make-up is removed, she watches the film. She analyzes what could be better, then gives a report to every team, including herself. Lighting, sound, stage, vocals, dancers. What needs to be tweaked to go from good to great? I will never hold a candle to Beyonce as a performer, but I can use her practices to become a better presenter. Performer vs. presenter. We are all a little bit of both. Let's be the best.

What will you repeat? What will you alter for next time? What did you learn about yourself as a presenter? What did you learn about your participants? How can you use that information to make your next presentation better?  How can you improve youBe sure to start with the positive though.  Give yourself some kudos as well as some grace.  We tend to focus on what needs to change, instead of celebrating what went well.

## THE LEARNING CONTINUES

The learning does not have to stop here.  Let's continue on this journey together.  My social media sources have lots of tools, tips and tricks for success.  Those tips and tricks include my joining you to model these practices and teach alongside you.  I also have stories to share and interviews with other excellent facilitators of learning.  I hope you will continue to learn with me.

Visit:
LearningCanStick.com

Now, let's go sing some karaoke and knock their socks off.

# NEED TO KNOW

Revisit the objectives of the training at the end of the training and then again a few weeks later via a survey or brief conversation with participants.

Determine next steps with the leadership team. Work with them to decide what sort of follow up is logical.

Create a follow-up opportunity to refresh the information. The more we drip, drip, drip the more people are likely to utilize the new learning.

Reflect on the experience personally. Growth happens when we create the space to learn from our experiences.

# NOTE-TAKING

Go back through your notes from this book to determine what your next steps might be. Make a list of things you would like to try, then give yourself the space to try one or two. You do not have to try it all, but each time you try one new technique the learning will get stickier.

Summarize your overall learning into three sentences.

# NEXT STEPS

Go be awesome! I can't wait to hear all about it. Let me know how it went on my socials.

Instagram: @learningcanstick          Facebook: Learning Can Stick

Twitter: @learningcanstick

# END NOTES

## Introduction

Aguilar, E. (2018). Mind-the-Gap [Pdf]. Oakland: Bright Morning.

## Chapter 1

Dweck, C. (2017). Decades of Scientific Research that Started a Growth Mindset Revolution. Retrieved May 21, 2020, from https://www.mindsetworks.com/science/

Makhlouf, J. (2019, September 20). Pedagogy vs. Andragogy: Where Many Get it Wrong In Their Learning Strategy. Retrieved April 5, 2020, from https://elmlearning.com/pedagogy-vs-andragogy/

Westland, J. (2020, July 02). The Triple Constraint in Project Management: Time, Scope & Cost. Retrieved March 13, 2020, from https://www.projectmanager.com/blog/triple-constraint-project-management-time-scope-cost

Andriotis, N. (2019, October 17). Learning Retention: 8 Proven Methods & Strategies to Recall Knowledge. Retrieved April 3, 2020, from https://www.talentlms.com/blog/8-tips-techniques-learning-retention/

Gutierrez, K. (2017, August 22). Mind-blowing Statistics that Prove the Value of Employee Training and Development. Retrieved July 21, 2020, from https://www.shiftelearning.com/blog/statistics-value-of-employee-training-and-development

Briceño, E. (Director). (2016). How to get better at the things you care about [Video file]. Retrieved July 21, 2020, from https://www.ted.com/talks/eduardo_briceno_how_to_get_better_at_the_things_you_care_about/footnotes?referrer=playlist-how_to_survive_following_your_passions

Kotter, J. P. (2012). Leading change. Boston, MA: Harvard Business School Press.

Fullan, M. (2011). The six secrets of change: What the best leaders do to help their organizations survive and thrive. San Francisco, CA, CA: Jossey-Bass.

Aguilar, E. (2018). Mind-the-Gap [Pdf]. Oakland: Bright Morning.

## Chapter 2

Brown, B. (2019). Dare to lead: Brave work, tough conversations, whole hearts. NY: Random House Large Print Publishing. (pg. 21)

Sinek, S. (2019). Start with why: How great leaders inspire everyone to take action. London, England: Penguin Business.

Dweck, C. (2017). Decades of Scientific Research that Started a Growth Mindset Revolution. Retrieved May 21, 2020, from https://www.mindsetworks.com/science/

Edwards, V. V. (2018). Captivate: The science of succeeding with people. New York, NY: Portfolio/Penguin.

## Chapter 5

Kotter, J. P. (2012). Leading change. Boston, MA: Harvard Business School Press.

Pontefract, D. (2019, September 15). The Wasted Dollars Of Corporate Training Programs. Retrieved January 25, 2020, from https://www.forbes.com/sites/danpontefract/2019/09/15/the-wasted-dollars-of-corporate-training-programs/

Rogers, S. (1994). Teaching for excellence: Essential concepts, strategies, techniques, and processes for ensuring performance excellence for all kids. Conifer, CO, CO: Peak Learning Systems.

Question mark art: http://www.pngall.com/question-mark-png/download/29911

# THANK YOU

Writing this book has been a true journey, and I have some very significant people to thank.

**Jason**, my incredible husband supported me through every late night, crazy idea, and need to vent. I love you.

**Chloe**, my talented daughter, hand wrote the fonts seen throughout this book on the cover and in the titles. She has such a gift and it is an honor to share it with the world.

**Jackson**, my brilliant son, is my marketing manager, and his work in this process is just beginning!

**Emily**, my dear life-long friend, made this book come to life with her amazing art! I love that she told my story through pictures!

**Robin**, my mentor and friend, read and edited many drafts to get me to today's version. I appreciate her willingness to guide me every single day.

**Kristen, Brandi, Tara, Tiffany, Sarah, and Kerrale**, my people, who read through the final version and made it even better!

**Kelsey and Caley**, my exercise buddies, genuinely listened and encouraged me as I shared this journey on our long runs and after exercise prayers.

**My entire family and all my friends** believed in me and showed me support and love throughout the process.

**Two Penny Publishing** guided me to a finished product that makes me incredibly proud. Tom unleashed my superpower then built a team of editors and artists to make the book exactly what I wanted. Jodi was absolutely incredible. Thank you for making my book come to life.

# AUTHOR

Dr. Christie L. McMullen spent the last 20+ years as an educator but has spent her entire life as a learner. Learning Can Stick grew out of decades of observations and trial and error in learning environments. Christie loves making people laugh while they learn and recognized early on that evoking emotion increases retention of information. She transitioned from teaching high school to teaching adults early in her career and has worked with adult learners in many settings. Whether training educators, business leaders, medical personnel, or her own children, she knows that learning sticks when it is safe, logical, fun, and memorable. She might even convince you that adults need stickers too.

Becoming Dr. Christie L. McMullen
with husband, Jason McMullen.

Throughout this book she shares stories and experiences related to every type of learning situation. Whether training one on one, in small groups or working with hundreds of people at a time, she knows how to make the experience worthwhile. Her goal is to transfer that knowledge to you, so that you will reinforce her motto that professional learning does not have to be painful.

Made in the USA
Middletown, DE
20 February 2024

49893972R00097